FLYING BIRD
ORIGAMI

YOSHIHIDE MOMOTANI

Published by Seibundo Shinkosha Publishing Co., Ltd.
13-7, Yayoicho 1-chome, Nakano-ku, Tokyo, 164 Japan

Distributors:
UNITED STATES: *Kodansha America, Inc., through Farrar, Straus & Giroux, 19 Union Square West, New York, NY 10003.*
CANADA: *Fitzhenry & Whiteside Ltd., 91 Granton Drive, Richmond Hill, Ontario L4B 2N5.*
BRITISH ISLES AND EUROPEAN CONTINENT: *Premier Book Marketing Ltd., 1 Gower Street, London WC1E 6HA.*
AUSTRALIA AND NEW ZEALAND: *Bookwise International, 54 Crittenden Road, Findon, South Australia 5023.*
THE FAR EAST AND JAPAN: *Japan Publications Trading Co., Ltd., 1-2-1, Sarugaku-cho, Chiyoda-ku, Tokyo 101.*

First edition: April 1993

ISBN 0-87040-908-5

Printed in Japan

Cut-and-insert origami ① Crane (p.22)   ② Blue Magpie (p.30)   ③ Dove B (p.26)   ④ Peregrine Falcon (p.27)
⑤ Korean Magpie (p.29)   ⑥ Pheasant (p.24)   ⑦ Firebird (p.28)

Birds of the forest ①Bulbul (p.44) ②Pale Ouzel (p.62) ③Woodpecker B (p.67) ④Cuckoo
⑤Siberian Blue Robin (p.64) ⑥Bush Warbler ⑦Woodpecker A (p.66)

4

River and lake birds ①Mallard ②Mallard ③Saberbill (p.52) ④Duck C (p.55)
⑤Ibis ⑥Wagtail B (p.45) ⑦Swan C (p.57)

Seabirds ①Albatross ②Seagull C (p.48) ③Frigate Bird
④Pelican ⑤Swift

6 Birds without page numbers are for reference only.

Contents

    A Word About Shape／Requirements
for Flight／Conditions for Flight／
Paper Size ／ Paper ／ Balance of
Shape／Bilateral Symmetry／Center
of Gravity ／ Tail Size ／ Upward
Curving Angle／Wing Load／Flapping
Wings ／ Center of Wind Pressure／
Stationary Stability, Restabilizing
Ability, Stability in Motion／Fixing
the Shape ／ Test Flight ／ Stalling／
Flying Method

Contents

A Word About Shape

Using origami (folded paper) to recreate the beautiful, flowing lines of a bird's shape is not easy, simply because when you fold paper, you get straight lines. Therefore, to create the illusion of curves, several straight lines are used together.

What we have tried to do in this book is to gather together as many origami methods and shapes of birds as possible. We begin with simple paper airplane applications and as we work up to more complicated designs, we apply flight requirements as they relate to the different bird shapes. By the end we present how to make 3-dimensional designs and furthermore give details on how to make them fly successfully.

Basically, by applying variations to one origami design one can fold a wide variety of bird shapes. Certainly that is the easiest way to learn. However in terms of expressing the beauty of birds, that alone is not enough.

Let's consider for example, the drawing of a picture of a bird. Depending on the person, their way of capturing the shape of a bird with differ. There will be people who love heavy lines, those who are skilled at drawing little details, and those who create something like a comic-book drawing. In this way, the very same bird, being represented by different drawing styles can also be expressed through myriad styles of origami.

Requirements for Flight

Birds fly in a lot of different ways. Even when they are gliding, and not flapping their wings, they are making small adjustments with their wings and tail to change direction. In order for paper planes to continue gliding well, even if they lean in the wind, they need enough stability to right themselves into their original direction.

Real birds do not just use their tails but also their feet and their long necks to maintain stability. For that reason, paper airplanes need to have a larger tail area than birds do.

In the same way, when making origami birds that fly, if the tail area is not larger than the real bird being represented, it will not have the stability required to glide well. I took great pains on this point though, because a tail that is too large looks unnatural.

A tailless plane has just one large set of wings that also serve the function a tail. This arrangement is not good for leaning into the wind, but flies very well in calm air. Folded paper birds can also be planned with this quality, and they come out somewhat resembling the real thing, with small tails.

Wing

Tail

Wings and tail

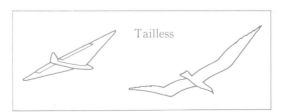

Tailless

Conditions for Flight

In the course of folding origami birds, there are so many folds to make, it is easy to make a careless mistake. We can correct the mistake, but then the paper becomes crumpled and these crumples add to the air resistance. For that reason, please be sure to fold every bird design more than twice.

The first time, fold it to understand the folding order and then fold it again with a new sheet of paper, avoiding any re-folding along the way. If you do that you will be able to make one that flies well. When you have folded a design that you have thought up yourself, and it looks good and has a properly placed center of gravity but for some reason does not fly well, by all means do fold it again using a new sheet of paper.

Folding and refolding an origami bird many times will undoubtedly disfigure it. It will definitely not fly straight if its beak gets bent, since the beak functions as a rudder, so you should straighten it out once in a while. The main crease along the torso also tends to spread out after being flown a lot, which also adds to air resistance. This is true for most paper airplanes too. Therefore, extra care should be made to make that main crease of the body firmly so that it does nor open up easily.

The birds in this book are folded so that their bodies stay closed. When creating your own flying bird origami designs, you ought to keep this in mind.

Paper Size

Paper that is about the size of your stretched-out hand is easy to fold, but it is difficult for children to fold paper the size of their hands because their hands are so small. Also, when cutting ordinary paper down to smaller pieces, keep in mind the effect of the paper's elasticity and hardness and the fact that it is difficult to cut things accurately. These factors are bound to affect how your origami flies.

Especially in the case of small children, since their hands are not yet strong enough to make firm creases, it is a good idea for them to use thinner paper which is larger than their hands. Sometimes flying bird origami made with large pieces of paper lack strength. This is particularly true of the base of the wing which bears much of the weight and is apt to lose its shape in flight so you will want to make that angle especially strong. Naturally then it is wise to use heavier paper: the larger the design, the heavier the gauge of paper. However, when you are making very large designs, even if the paper is thicker, it may not be firm enough.

As an example, supposing we make the paper twice the size, and double the thickness, the overall weight will increase by 8 times, so even though the paper is thicker, it will not be sufficiently strong to hold the shape and fly. Therefore, for large designs, insert wooden bones to add support.

On the contrary, if you use thin, small-sized paper it will fly better because there is less load per wing area. Of course if you use a paper which is too small, it is harder to fold, and may not look as good.

Paper

The best paper for origami has low elasticity, has no extra ripples and makes a distinct crease. Aluminum foil is good for making and keeping its crease, but it tends to have excessive unevenness. Paper with a layer of aluminum foil stuck to it is good for making creases and holds its shape well, but its drawback is that it is quite heavy in relation to its solidness.

Normally Japanese paper is considered good for origami, but the problems it presents for flying bird origami are that its rough surface causes some wind drag and the creases lose their shape after a while. The paper best used for the designs in this book is standard, good quality paper of between 15 and 20cm (8 and 12 inches) square.

Balance of Shape

In order to recreate birds, one must capture aspects of their beauty such as their color and shape. At the same time, since origami is made up of straight lines, an impressive shape relies not only on realistic elements but also on seizing the beauty of a bird in the abstract sense.

Given the numerous technical restrictions intrinsic to origami, I am not sure how far I can go with its depth of expression, but origami does have one great merit and that is that I can improve bit by bit by folding a design as many times as I like.

I think that one main aspect of playful experimentation with origami is in the balance between color and shape. For example there is paper with white on one side only that can be used to face out for specific parts, and different weights and thickness of folds give various effects.

Bilateral Symmetry

Considerations of beauty aside, one of the conditions for making something that flies well is that of functional balance. As a general rule then, when seen directly from the front and from overhead, the shape should be bilaterally symmetrical.

Center of Gravity

The point of support that allows a plane to stay horizontal is the center of gravity. A plane with rectangular wings will fly well if its center of gravity is about 1/3 or 2/5 from the front of the wings. If the tail has lift, put the center of gravity about 1/2 or 2/3 the distance from the front of the wings.

This is fundamental, so for instance to create the same conditions with a sweptback wing, think of the overall wing area as seen from above and place the center of gravity about 1/3 of the way from the front of the wings.

Usually in model airplanes, weight is added to the nose to help adjust the center of gravity but the birds in this book are folded by placing the weight efficiently from the start. This way of making each origami fold in an intentional way, without adding anything in the process has been one of the ground rules of the art since olden times.

Tail Size

Gliding ability is good when the center of gravity is 1/3 the distance from the front edge of the wings. The horizontal tail provides stability which keeps the nose from pointing up or down and the vertical tail portion of model airplanes keeps the nose from swinging sideways. For the birds in this book, the rear half of the body serves the same function as this vertical wing. Although a larger tail does increase stability, it does not add much to the length of flight so it is probably best to make the tail not overly large but just suitably large for the bird.

Stability increases when the tail is the farthest possible distance from the main wing, however to be true to the shape of real birds, we can only add large tails if they are for peacocks or pheasants.

It is possible to minimize the appearance of the tail by having the rear part of the torso and the neck perform the same function as the tail. Keep this in mind when you are creating new designs, too.

Upward Curving Angle

Looking at the wings of a model plane from the front, you see that the wings are tilted slightly upwards, which helps prevent the body of the plane from veering left and right.

Without this upward curve, paper airplanes tend to roll. Actually, even when the upward curve is insufficient, if the body is situated below the wings, the stability will be good. In fact when a bird is flying, it circles toward the right or left by dipping the tip of its wing down.

Wing Load

Wing load is what we call the weight falling on a given wing area. The heavier the wing load, the greater the lift per unit of wing area is needed. This is aided by flying fast, providing air resistance is low. A bird with large wings in relation to its body can fly slowly because its wing load is low.

Origami flying birds can glide a long time when the wing load is decreased, as it is with large, light wings.

Flapping Wings

There is a way that you can make wings that flap, by twisting down the front edge about 1/3 the distance from the wingtip. However, to maintain stability, twist up the rear edge or it will want to plunge downwards.

The flapping of the wings is caused by the unstable flow of air around the wings but it does not always occur, depending on the stiffness or angle of the wings. If it does work, it is interesting indeed, though of course the flapping does not help it fly.

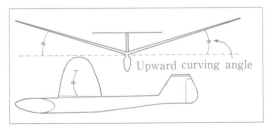

Upward curving angle

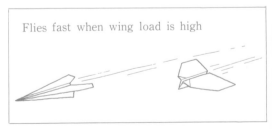

Flies fast when wing load is high

Center of Wind Pressure

When something is thrown, air resistance occurs. The center of air resistance will differ depending on the shape of the object. If the center of wind pressure pushing the object backwards does not coincide with the center of gravity of the object, the object will change direction.

If the center of air resistance is located ahead of the center of gravity, it will not fly straight because the front and rear will tend to go in different directions. If anything, it may fall, spiralling downwards. When the center of air resistance is located behind the center of gravity, it should fly straight but there is a set of conditions, as described below.

Stationary Stability, Restabilizing Ability, Stability in Motion

If the center of air resistance is located behind the center of gravity, the power to restore its original direction acts as soon as it is pushed off course. By doing that, the power to restabilize and return to straight ahead actually becomes too much and its tail shakes back and forth. In fact, sometimes as this tail swing grows in intensity the plane will no longer fly. Also, if the wings are angled upwards too much, the plane will tend to veer left or right.

Depending on the type of bird, we can use these flight characteristics to our advantage when making paper birds. For instance an origami swallow made with a big tail will meander left and right as it flies. If a paper bird whose tail is obscured by its wings and body rolls onto its side, it will fall into a nose spin. What is needed for maintaining gliding stability is an adequate balance of both stationary stability, which keeps it steady, and restabilizing ability in case it is knocked off course.

Fixing the Shape

When you have folded a paper bird, look at it from straight above to check its bilateral symmetry. When you fold the wings together overhead, they should lie precisely in line with each other. If this is not the case, adjust the fold so that they do line up. The place where the wings attach is where the most pressure is applied so we must be careful not to re-fold this crease too many times or it will weaken, causing the wings to fold up in flight. Secondly, when you mend the wings, make sure that they have the same upward curving angle when seen from the front.

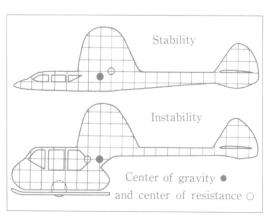

Stability

Instability

Center of gravity ●
and center of resistance ○

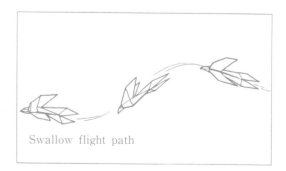

Swallow flight path

Test Flight

At first, try releasing the bird by pushing it out lightly, straight and slightly down from horizontal. Take careful note of how it flies. If it nose-dives right when you let go of it, maybe you should throw it harder. Also if it flies upwards, try throwing it a little slower. If it flies straight and slightly downwards from the point when it leaves your hand, it is going just the right speed.

The flight speed changes according to the way it has been folded. To avoid curves to the right and left, be sure that the upward angle of the wings is equal, and that the tail and beak are both straight.

Even when thrown hard, if it nose-dives rather than rising up, then the center of gravity can come forward. Try adjusting the wing position a bit forward as seen from directly above or bend the tip of the tail up a bit. Furthermore, if the body has a horizontal flat part to it, and the front of the wings are a little raised up creating an angle of attack, it is less apt to plunge.

Stalling

If you have folded a bird correctly, it will be as on the left, but if it flies making an up and down wavelike action, or goes up a bit and then crashes suddenly down then the center of gravity is too far back or the wings are too far forward or the sweptback angle of the wings is not enough. When it is difficult to fix an origami bird, try just bending the end of the tail down a bit and it will fly straight.

Flying Method

Throwing a bird with all of your force does not help. There is a bit of a knack to releasing it from your hand so it flies straight out. Practice throwing so that it starts off leaning a bit to the right or left and rises spiraling to horizontal in flight. This is helpful for flight endurance contests!

This works successfully only when all the various factors, like the leaning angle, the power to restore stability, throwing speed, and upward angle are all fine, so until you get used to this method of flying, you may find it quite difficult.

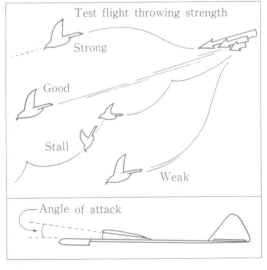

Test flight throwing strength

Strong

Good

Stall

Weak

Angle of attack

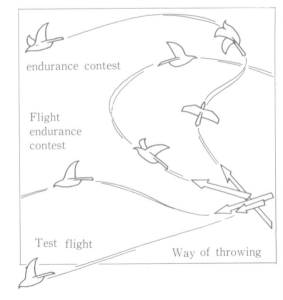

endurance contest

Flight endurance contest

Test flight

Way of throwing

METHODS OF FOLDING
FLYING BIRD ORIGAMI

Origami Methods and Symbols

(some common examples)

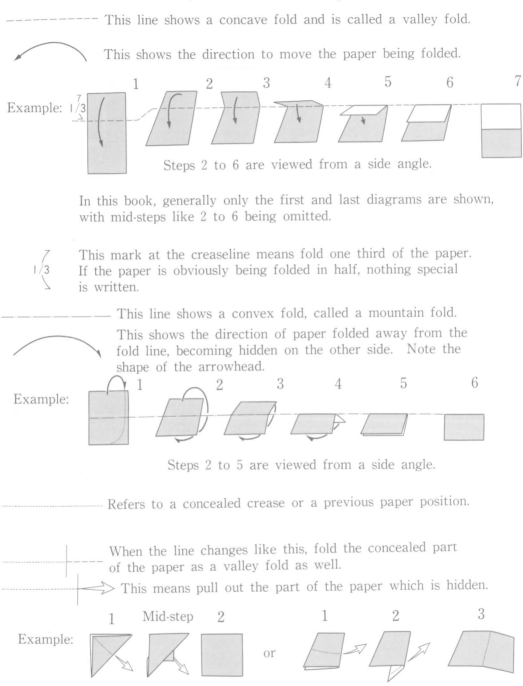

—————————— This line shows a concave fold and is called a valley fold.

This shows the direction to move the paper being folded.

Example: 1/3

1   2   3   4   5   6   7

Steps 2 to 6 are viewed from a side angle.

In this book, generally only the first and last diagrams are shown, with mid-steps like 2 to 6 being omitted.

1/3   This mark at the creaseline means fold one third of the paper. If the paper is obviously being folded in half, nothing special is written.

— — — — — — This line shows a convex fold, called a mountain fold.

This shows the direction of paper folded away from the fold line, becoming hidden on the other side. Note the shape of the arrowhead.

Example:

1   2   3   4   5   6

Steps 2 to 5 are viewed from a side angle.

·················· Refers to a concealed crease or a previous paper position.

When the line changes like this, fold the concealed part of the paper as a valley fold as well.

This means pull out the part of the paper which is hidden.

1   Mid-step   2   1   2   3

Example: or

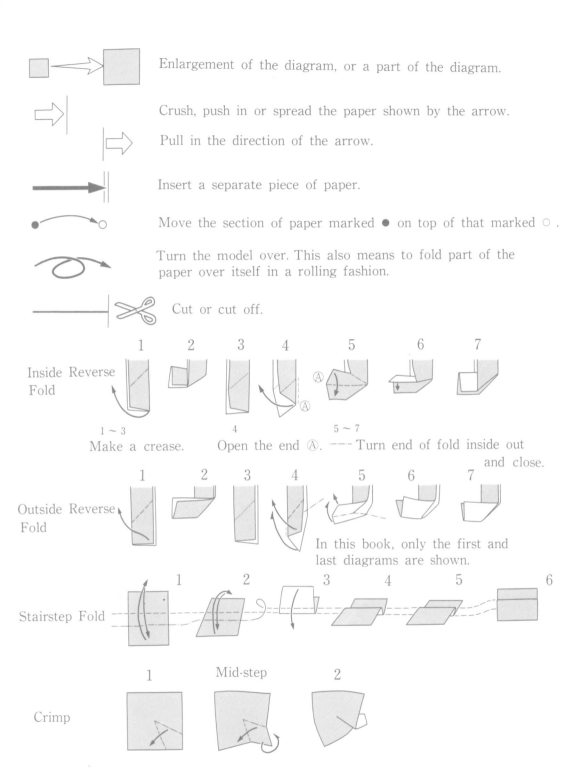

Enlargement of the diagram, or a part of the diagram.

Crush, push in or spread the paper shown by the arrow.

Pull in the direction of the arrow.

Insert a separate piece of paper.

Move the section of paper marked ● on top of that marked ○.

Turn the model over. This also means to fold part of the paper over itself in a rolling fashion.

Cut or cut off.

Inside Reverse Fold

1   2   3   4   5   6   7

1 ~ 3   4   5 ~ 7
Make a crease.   Open the end Ⓐ. ----Turn end of fold inside out
                                              and close.

Outside Reverse Fold

1   2   3   4   5   6   7

In this book, only the first and last diagrams are shown.

Stairstep Fold

1   2   3   4   5   6

Crimp

1   Mid-step   2

Folding Method Basics (An example of the inside reverse fold)

Swan A

This paper airplane design has been around a long time. The center of gravity of most paper airplanes is in the middle (see step 6), with the nose of the plane shaped like an arrow.

A fold to this plane's neck gives us Swan A. With its wings folded up and its center of gravity forward, it flies well. It makes perfect sense to make this swan out of white paper, but we have used colored paper for purposes of clarity.

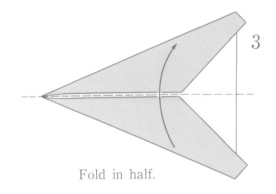

3

Fold in half.

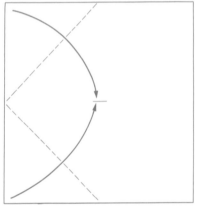

1

Bring corners to center.

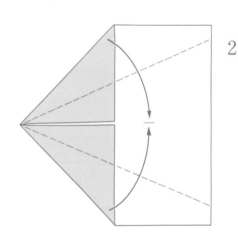

2

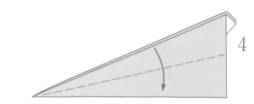

4

Fold over this one side only.

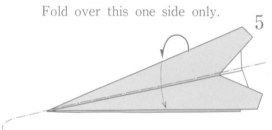

5

Fold top over to far side.

Center of gravity

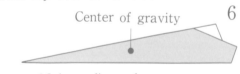

6

Make a firm, clean crease, then open wings horizontally.

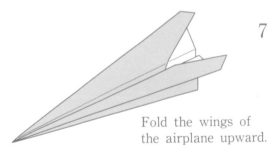

7

Fold the wings of the airplane upward.

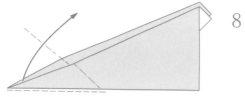

8

Open the point and fold it
in between the opened wings.

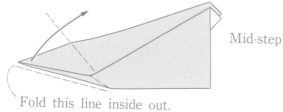

Mid-step

Fold this line inside out.

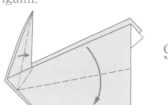

Mid-step

Close the point.
This fold, in steps 8 to 9,
called an inside reverse fold,
is one of the most important
folds in origami.

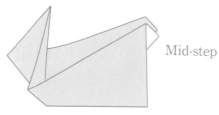

9

Make the small arrow fold as
you fold the large arrow fold.

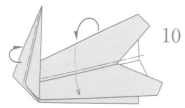

10

Do the same on the other side.

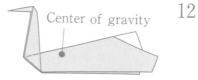

11

Make an inside reverse
fold to the tip only.

12

Center of gravity

Open the wings horizontally.

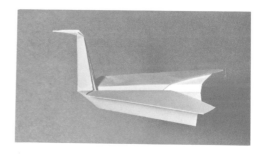

13

Finished Swan A

The explanations are very thorough here,
but in the rest of this book they will be
more brief. For example, in steps 4, 5
and 6, 5 would be left out, and in steps 8
and 9, the mid-step diagrams would also
be omitted.

Swan B

Like Swan A, Swan B is also based on a paper plane design, but it looks more like a real swan. The center of gravity is further back and the wing loading is less, so it flies slower.

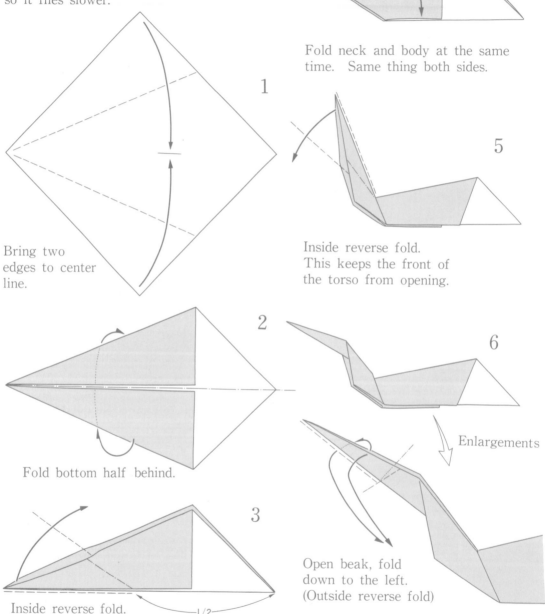

1

Bring two edges to center line.

4

Fold neck and body at the same time. Same thing both sides.

5

Inside reverse fold. This keeps the front of the torso from opening.

2

Fold bottom half behind.

6

Enlargements

3

Inside reverse fold.　—1/2—

Open beak, fold down to the left. (Outside reverse fold)

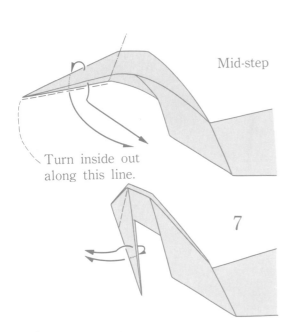

Mid-step

Turn inside out
along this line.

7

Open tip and fold inside out.
This is called an outside
reverse fold, one of the most
important folds in origami.

8

Pull inside of beak up.

9

Shorten with two
inside reverse folds.

10

Reduction

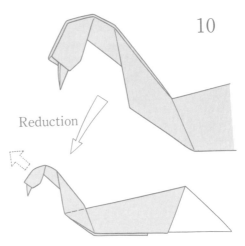

To turn the head down,
pull in direction of
the arrow, and open
wings horizontally.

11

Finished Swan B

In steps 5 & 10, keep the torso closed.
This is a key to making paper
airplanes that fly well.
As for steps 3 to 10, these neck folding
basics are very detailed, so practice
them many times. In step 4, you fold
two different parts at the same time,
which is a very helpful technique.

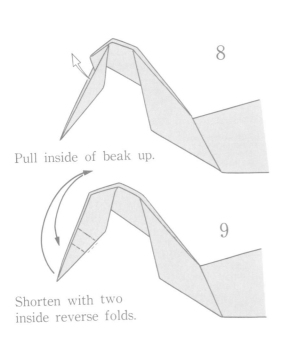

Simple Bird Method (Cut-and-insert origami)

Crane

Swan B on the previous page shows how to make a neck. On this page, the neck and front of the body are folded together and the rest of the body is made using a cutting method. This method can be applied to many other kinds of birds, too.

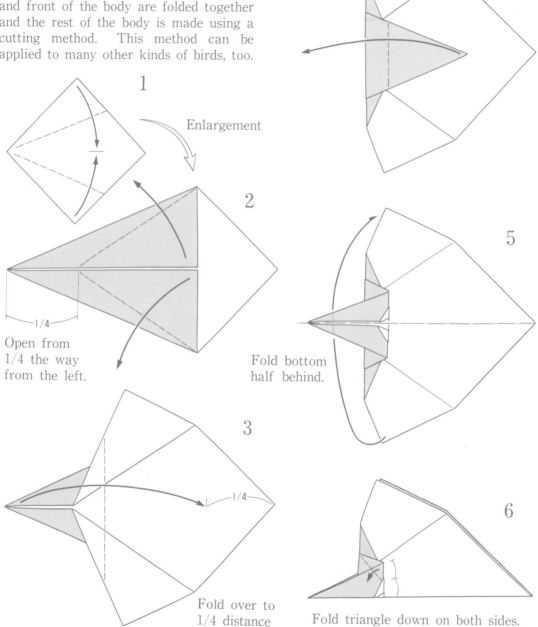

1

Enlargement

2

Open from 1/4 the way from the left.

3

Fold over to 1/4 distance from right.

4

5

Fold bottom half behind.

6

Fold triangle down on both sides.

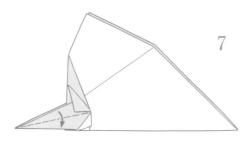

7

(It is best to fold 6 and 7 simultaneously.)

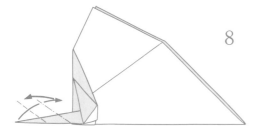

8

Two inside reverse folds to neck. (Stairstep fold)

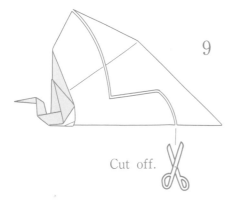

9

Cut off.

Stretch here a bit.

10

Wing crease moves
forward to dashed line.

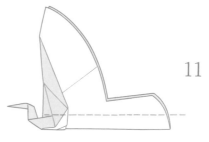

11

Spread wings.

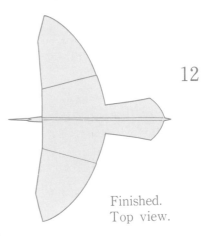

12

Finished.
Top view.

Pheasant

If you change how you cut, then also change the way you fold to match with what you have done. This of course will affect the way it flies, too.

A longer tail improves stability, but requires a longer neck too, allowing room to attach crest feathers.

Steps 1-4 here are the same as 1-8 of the Crane on the previous page, so they are simplified here.

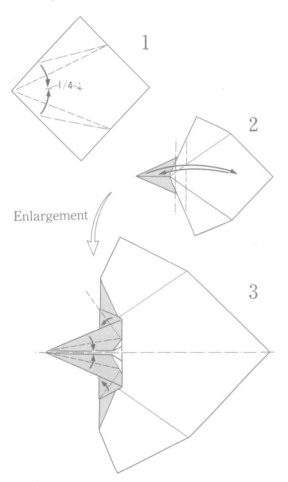

Enlargement

Fold the parts marked with arrows, then fold the bottom half behind.

(This point is the same as at step 8 of the Crane on the last page.)

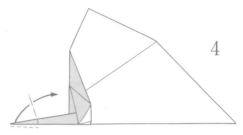

4

Inside reverse fold.

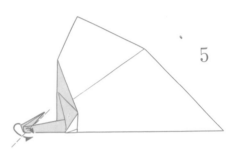

5

Open, make outside reverse fold. See step 6 for result.

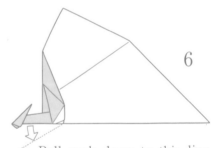

6

Pull neck down to this line.

Cut off as shown.

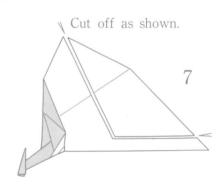

7

Flamingo

From step 4 on the left.

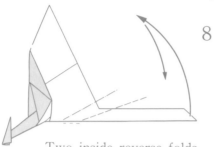

8

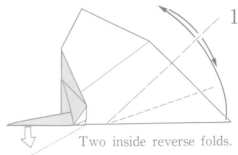

1

Two inside reverse folds.

Two inside reverse folds.

Pull neck down to this line.

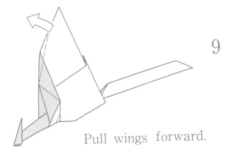

9

Cut, then pull wings forward.

2

Bend the neck as shown.

Pull wings forward.

Crimps.

10

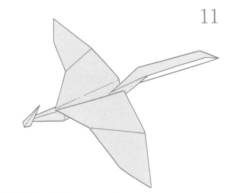

3

Spread wings.

Finished Flamingo.

11

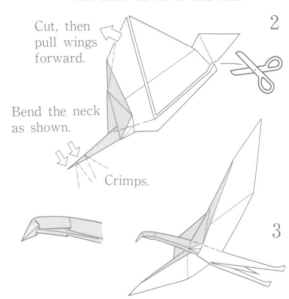

Finished Pheasant

Dove A

This cut-and-insert origami, passed down through the ages, is easy to make, but cannot fly in its original shape, so we alter it so that it can.

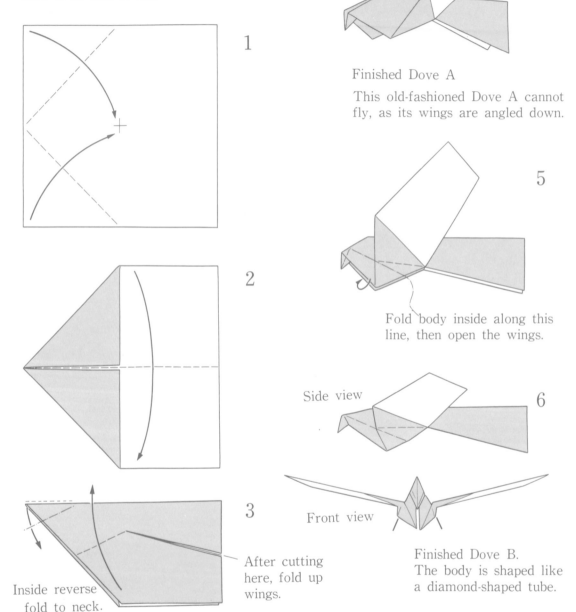

1

2

3

Inside reverse fold to neck.

After cutting here, fold up wings.

4

Finished Dove A

This old-fashioned Dove A cannot fly, as its wings are angled down.

5

Fold body inside along this line, then open the wings.

Side view

6

Front view

Finished Dove B.
The body is shaped like a diamond-shaped tube.

Peregrine Falcon

From step 3 on the left, re-open.

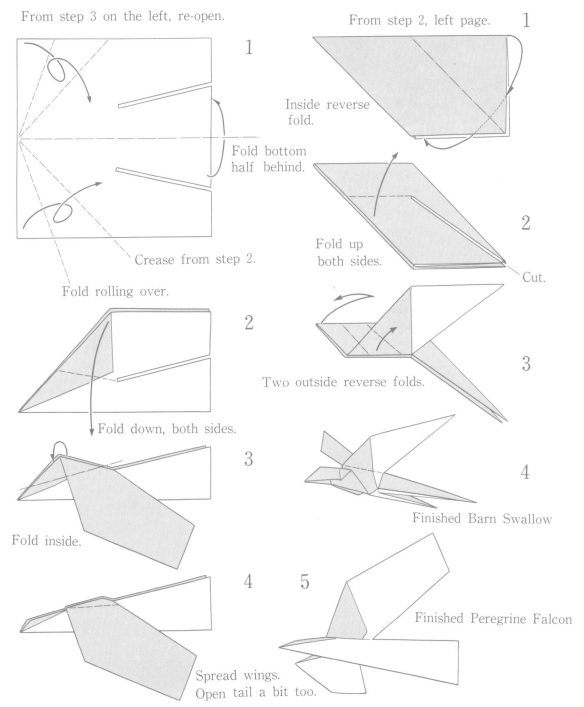

1

Fold bottom
half behind.

Crease from step 2.

Fold rolling over.

2

Fold down, both sides.

3

Fold inside.

4

Spread wings.
Open tail a bit too.

Barn Swallow

From step 2, left page.

1

Inside reverse
fold.

Fold up
both sides.

2

Cut.

Two outside reverse folds.

3

4

Finished Barn Swallow

5

Finished Peregrine Falcon

Firebird

Living in legend only, this bird was designed as imagined, with a lovely long neck and long tail.

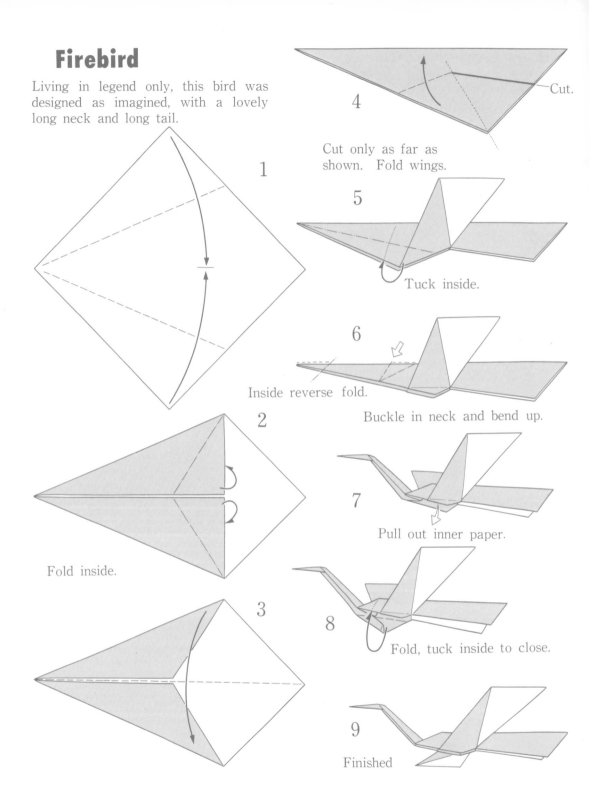

1

4

Cut.

Cut only as far as shown. Fold wings.

5

Tuck inside.

6

Inside reverse fold.

Buckle in neck and bend up.

2

Fold inside.

7

Pull out inner paper.

3

8

Fold, tuck inside to close.

9

Finished

Korean Magpie

Fold to step 3 on the left, then re-open.

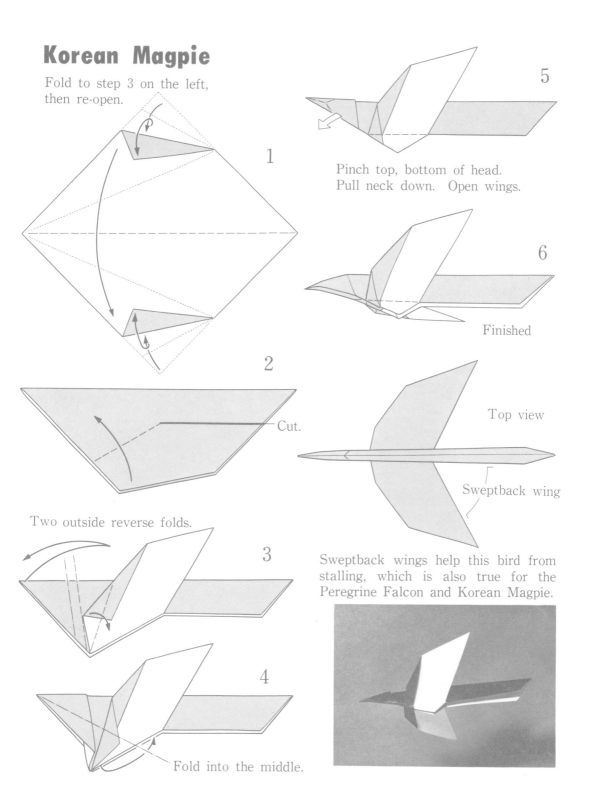

1

2

Cut.

Two outside reverse folds.

3

4

Fold into the middle.

5

Pinch top, bottom of head.
Pull neck down. Open wings.

6

Finished

Top view

Sweptback wing

Sweptback wings help this bird from stalling, which is also true for the Peregrine Falcon and Korean Magpie.

Blue Magpie

First fold paper triangle.

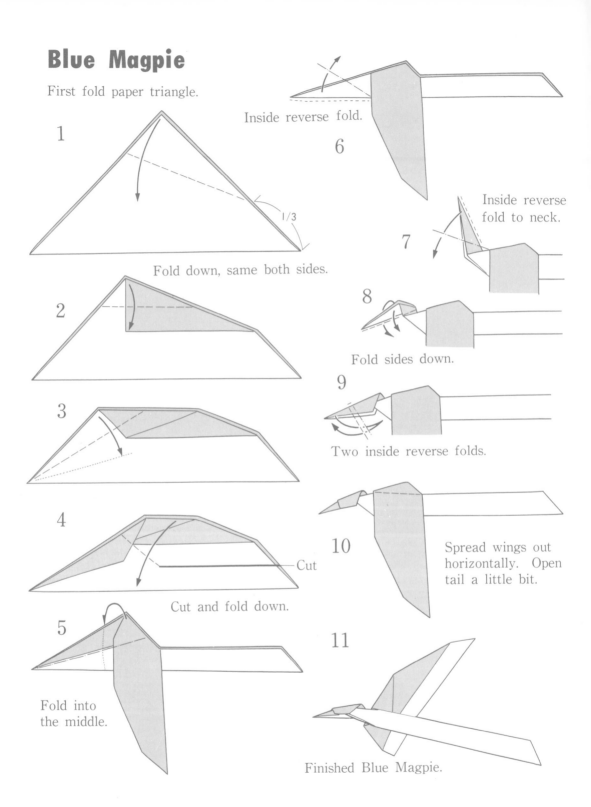

1 Fold down, same both sides. 1/3

2 Fold down, same both sides.

3

4 Cut — Cut and fold down.

5 Fold into the middle.

6 Inside reverse fold.

7 Inside reverse fold to neck.

8 Fold sides down.

9 Two inside reverse folds.

10 Spread wings out horizontally. Open tail a little bit.

11 Finished Blue Magpie.

Wagtail A

(See pg. 45 for Wagtail B)

This design combines a folded paper design and a cut paper design. It cannot fly because of its wings, but this wing design will be referred to later, so it is included here.

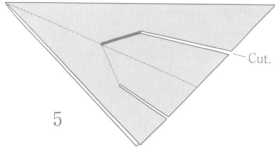

5

Cut dark line of crease only. Open and re-fold steps 1, 2, 3, 4. The wings are broader now because they are cut and no longer folded in half.

Cut.

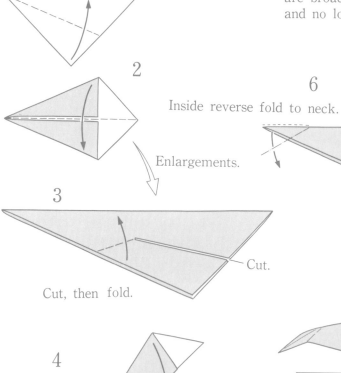

1

2

Enlargements.

3

Cut.

Cut, then fold.

4

Re-open as in step 1, then fold in half.

Inside reverse fold to neck.

6

Fold wings up.

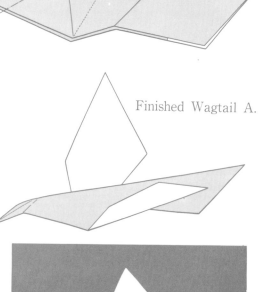

Finished Wagtail A.

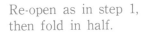

Flying Crane

This is the Crane design passed down through the ages, with an added device for moving the center of gravity forward.

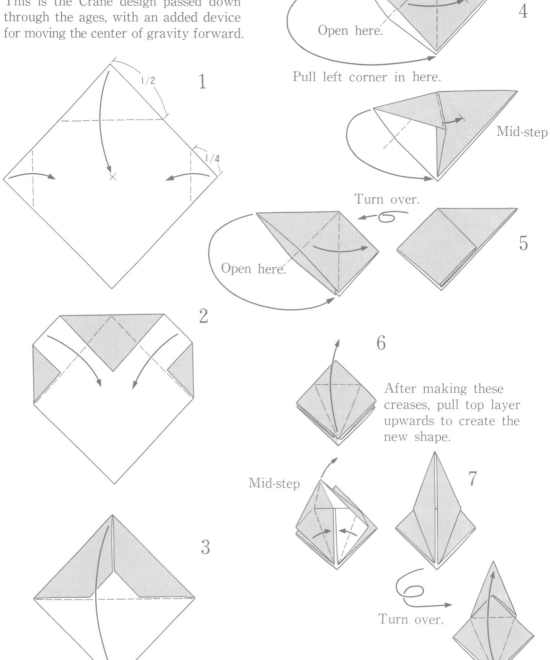

1

1/2

1/4

×

2

3

4

Open here.

Pull left corner in here.

Mid-step

Turn over.

Open here.

5

6

After making these creases, pull top layer upwards to create the new shape.

Mid-step

7

Turn over.

Flapping Wing Crane

Fold the Crane to step 8, then fold only the more thickly layered side.

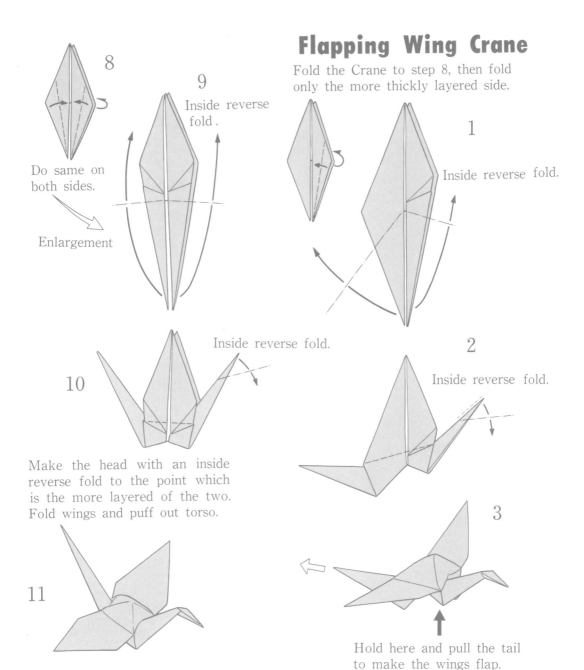

8

Do same on both sides.

Enlargement

9

Inside reverse fold.

1

Inside reverse fold.

10

Inside reverse fold.

Make the head with an inside reverse fold to the point which is the more layered of the two. Fold wings and puff out torso.

2

Inside reverse fold.

11

Finished Flying Crane.

3

Hold here and pull the tail to make the wings flap.

The original design omits steps 1 and 2, starting with a plain square paper at step 3.

This design has been around for a long time and by adding steps 1 & 2 on the left, became able to fly.

Peacock-like Crane

The front half of this bird is the same as the crane on the last page, but the back is like a fan.

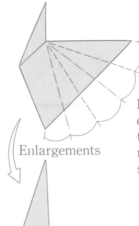

5

Fold both sides into 5 equal parts, reversing the order of valley and mountain folds from one side to the other.

Mid-step.

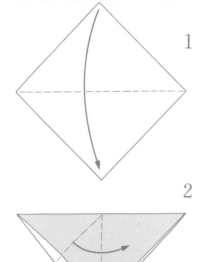

1

Open here.

2

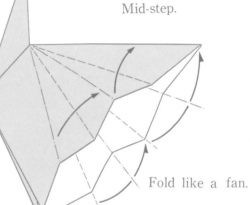

Fold like a fan.

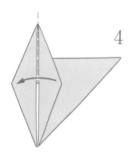

3

Fold up top layer only.

6

Fold up to open wings

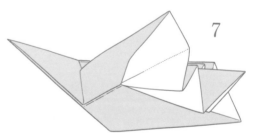

4

The Crane-like neck and wings are ready here. Make the base for the tail and wings, and after the tail, fold the last part of the neck.

7

Make same fold on other side too.

Peacock

(Application — cannot fly)

8

Fold wing and narrow fold to neck at the same time. Same to both sides.

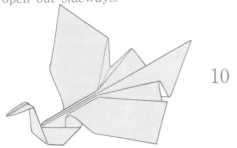

9

Make Two outside reverse folds to the neck. Be sure wings are not too angular open out sideways.

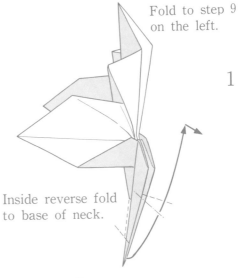

Fold to step 9 on the left.

1

Inside reverse fold to base of neck.

2

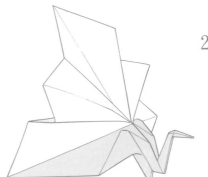

Finished Peacock.

10

Peacock like Crane.

In step 5, the number of equal sections does not have to be 5. This can be loosely interpreted as 7, or even 3 or 4. They also do not absolutely have to be even either, if you prefer otherwise.

Wild Goose A

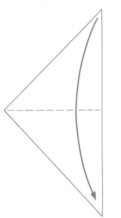

1

For a more light-weight design, cut the paper in half along the – – – – – line, (as was done in this case).

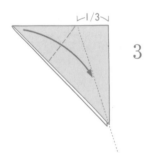

2

3

Left corner crosses to this measured angle.

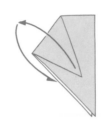

4

Steps 3 and 4 are for making a good crease, so re-open and re-fold to the other side as well.

5

Return to step 3

Enlargements

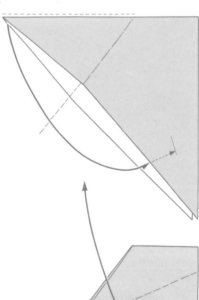

6

Make inside reverse fold along crease you just made.

Leaving this space, fold one layer up.

7

36

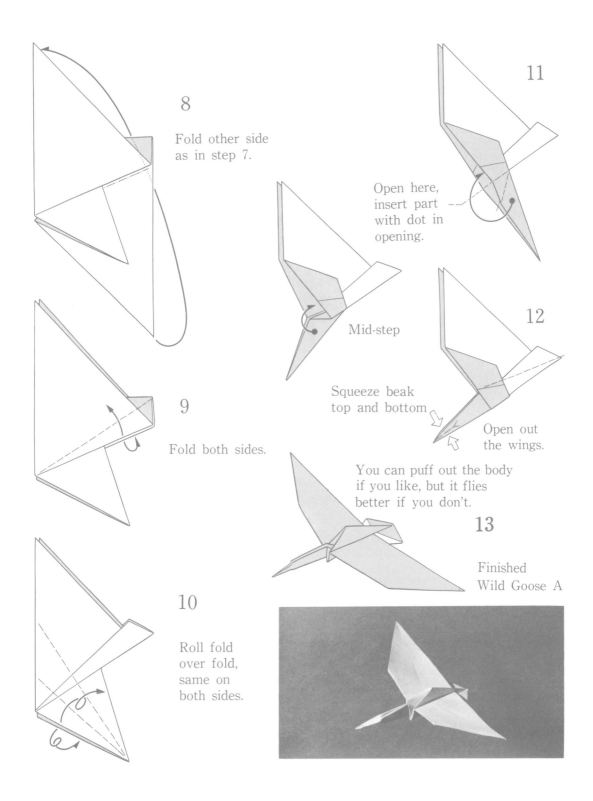

8

Fold other side as in step 7.

11

Open here, insert part with dot in opening.

Mid-step

9

Fold both sides.

12

Squeeze beak top and bottom

Open out the wings.

10

Roll fold over fold, same on both sides.

You can puff out the body if you like, but it flies better if you don't.

13

Finished Wild Goose A

Dove C

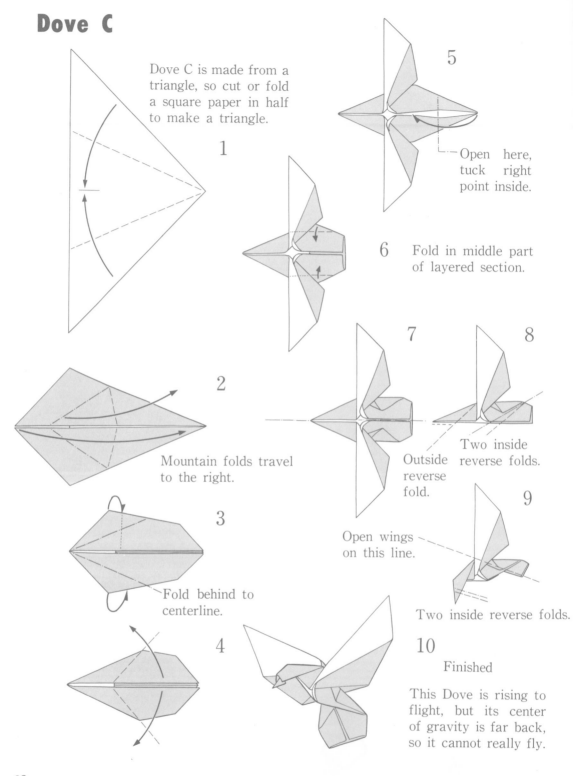

Dove C is made from a triangle, so cut or fold a square paper in half to make a triangle.

1

2

Mountain folds travel to the right.

3

Fold behind to centerline.

4

5

Open here, tuck right point inside.

6 Fold in middle part of layered section.

7

8

Outside reverse fold.

Two inside reverse folds.

Open wings on this line.

9

Two inside reverse folds.

10

Finished

This Dove is rising to flight, but its center of gravity is far back, so it cannot really fly.

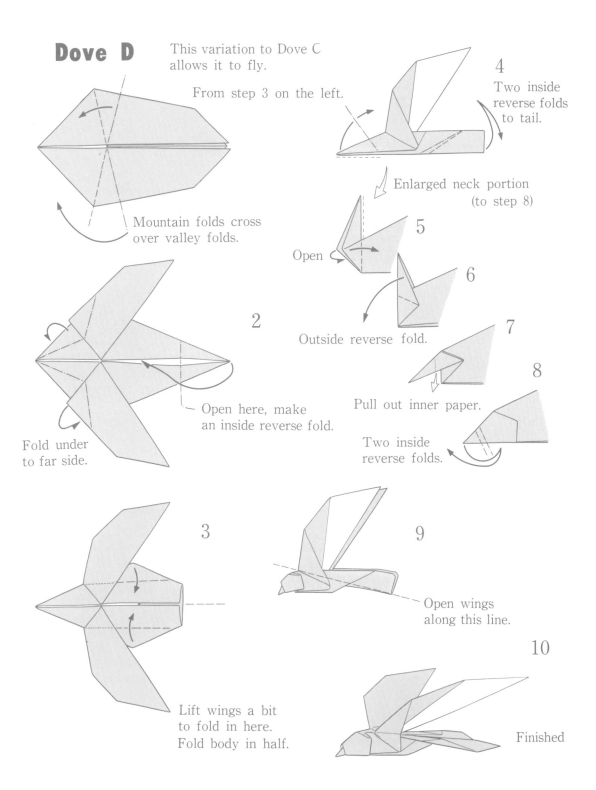

Dove D

This variation to Dove C allows it to fly.

From step 3 on the left.

4 Two inside reverse folds to tail.

Mountain folds cross over valley folds.

Enlarged neck portion (to step 8)

Open **5**

6

2

Outside reverse fold.

7

8

Open here, make an inside reverse fold.

Pull out inner paper.

Fold under to far side.

Two inside reverse folds.

3

9

Open wings along this line.

10

Lift wings a bit to fold in here. Fold body in half.

Finished

Wild Goose B

This is like a Dove C with the head and tail reversed. This is an example of how once you learn one pattern, it is easy to learn more.

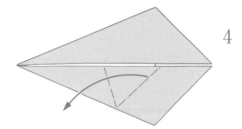

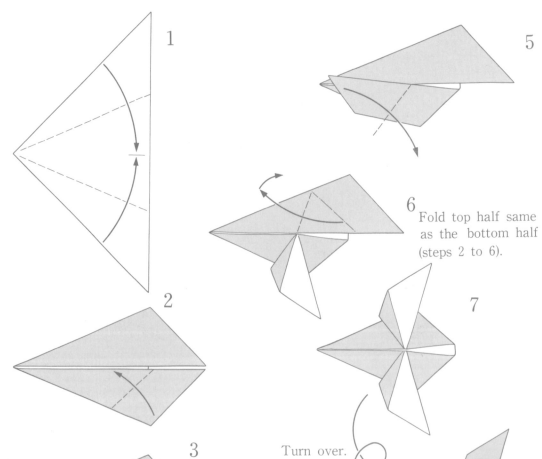

6 Fold top half same as the bottom half (steps 2 to 6).

Turn over.

Fold this just to make a crease, then re-open.

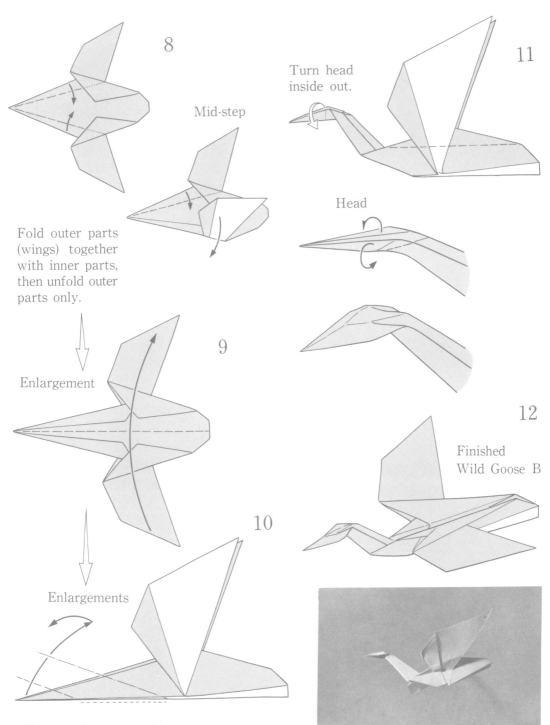

8

Mid-step

Fold outer parts (wings) together with inner parts, then unfold outer parts only.

Enlargement

9

Enlargements

10

Two inside reverse folds.

Turn head inside out.

11

Head

12

Finished Wild Goose B

Kingfisher

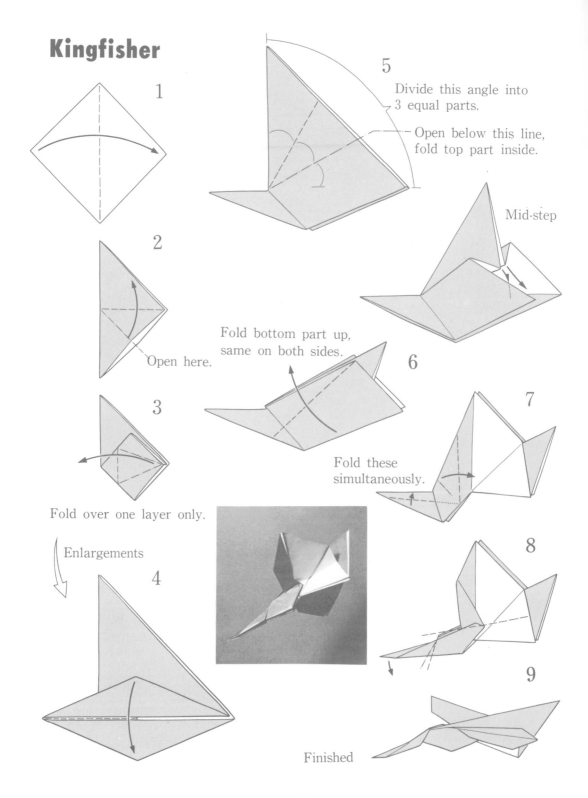

1

2

Open here.

3

Fold over one layer only.

Enlargements

4

5

Divide this angle into 3 equal parts.

Open below this line, fold top part inside.

Mid-step

Fold bottom part up, same on both sides.

6

7

Fold these simultaneously.

8

9

Finished

Little Bittern

From step 7, previous page.

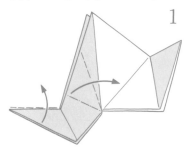

1

Lifting on the left,
fold the wing over.
Same to other side.

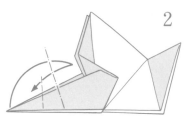

2

Two inside reverse folds.

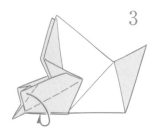

3

Fold over and insert
triangle inside.

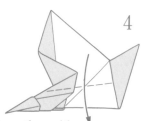

4

Same to other side.
Fold wings down.

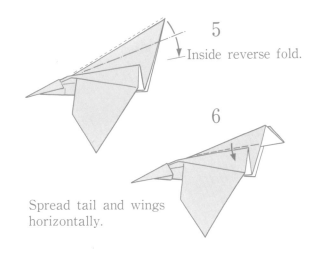

5

Inside reverse fold.

6

Spread tail and wings
horizontally.

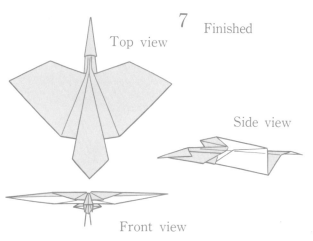

7 Finished

Top view

Side view

Front view

Bulbul

Steps 1-4 steps same as Kingfisher.

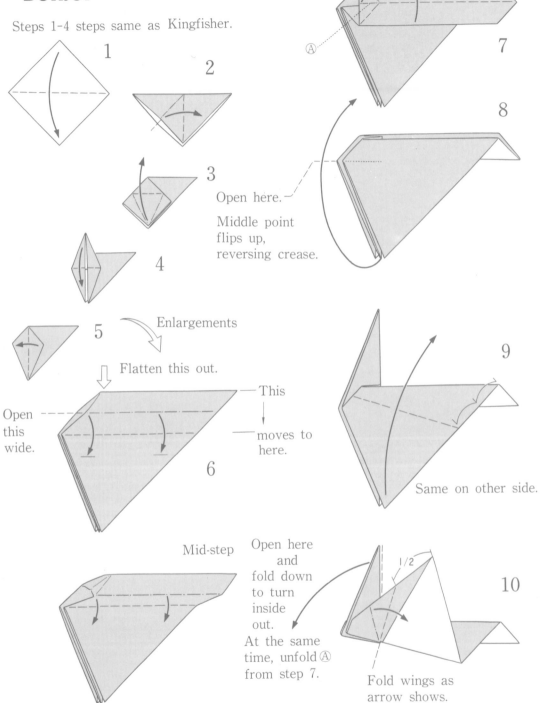

1

2

3

4

5 Enlargements

Flatten this out.

Open
this
wide.

This

moves to
here.

6

Open here.

Middle point
flips up,
reversing crease.

7

8

9

Same on other side.

Mid-step

Open here
and
fold down
to turn
inside
out.

At the same
time, unfold Ⓐ
from step 7.

10

1/2

Fold wings as
arrow shows.

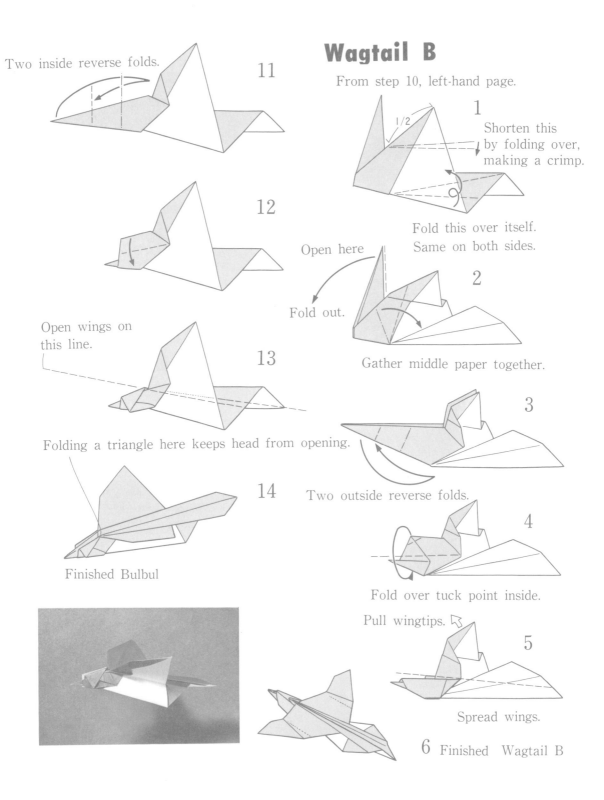

Two inside reverse folds. **11**

Wagtail B

From step 10, left-hand page. **1**

1/2

Shorten this by folding over, making a crimp.

Fold this over itself. Same on both sides.

12

Open here

Fold out.

2

Gather middle paper together.

Open wings on this line. **13**

Folding a triangle here keeps head from opening.

3

Two outside reverse folds.

14

4

Fold over tuck point inside.

Finished Bulbul

Pull wingtips.

5

Spread wings.

6 Finished Wagtail B

Seagull A

This Seagull consists of wings only. Birds that can stay in the air for a long time often have broad, long, wings. To fold paper birds that fly well, even more important than length and strength is an air resistance rate that gives lift. The wings on this page are one such example.

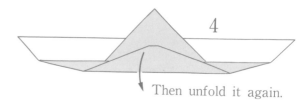

4

Then unfold it again.

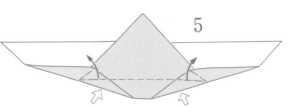

5

Distinguish —·—· lines from
– – – – – lines.
Push and fold so as to bring
—·—· lines up.

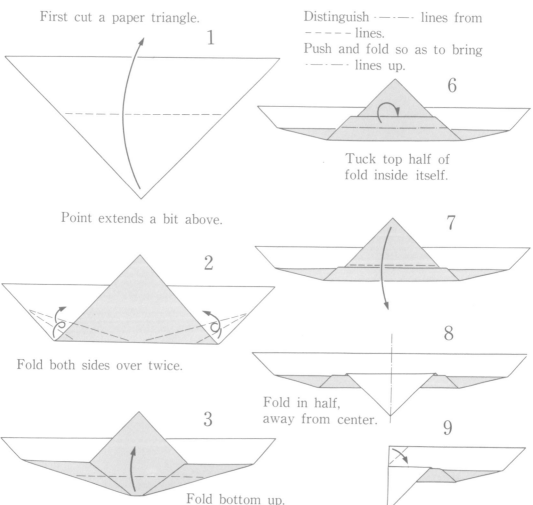

First cut a paper triangle.

1

Point extends a bit above.

2

Fold both sides over twice.

3

Fold bottom up.

6

Tuck top half of fold inside itself.

7

8

Fold in half, away from center.

9

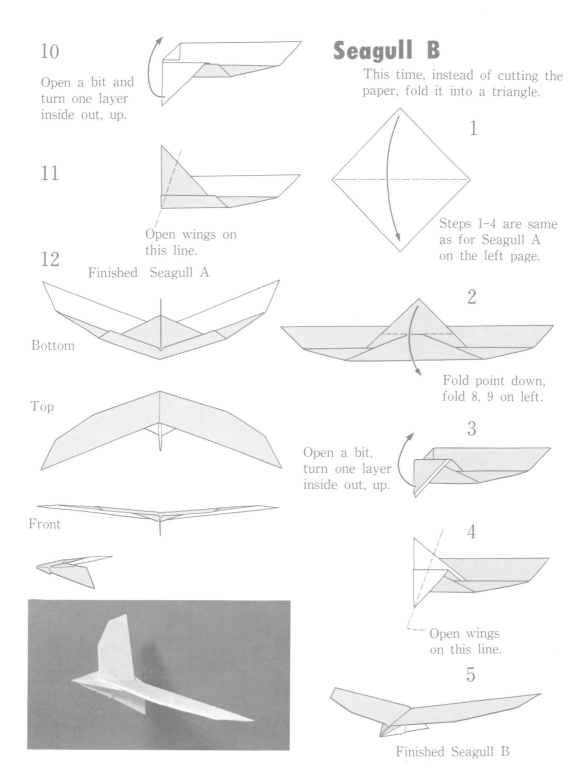

10

Open a bit and turn one layer inside out, up.

11

Open wings on this line.

12

Finished Seagull A

Bottom

Top

Front

Seagull B

This time, instead of cutting the paper, fold it into a triangle.

1

Steps 1-4 are same as for Seagull A on the left page.

2

Fold point down, fold 8, 9 on left.

3

Open a bit, turn one layer inside out, up.

4

Open wings on this line.

5

Finished Seagull B

Seagull C

This seagull looks more complete than Seagulls A and B because it also has a neck and tail.

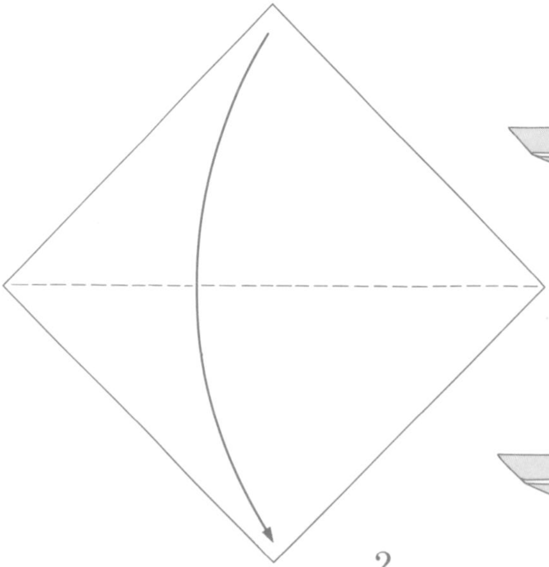

4

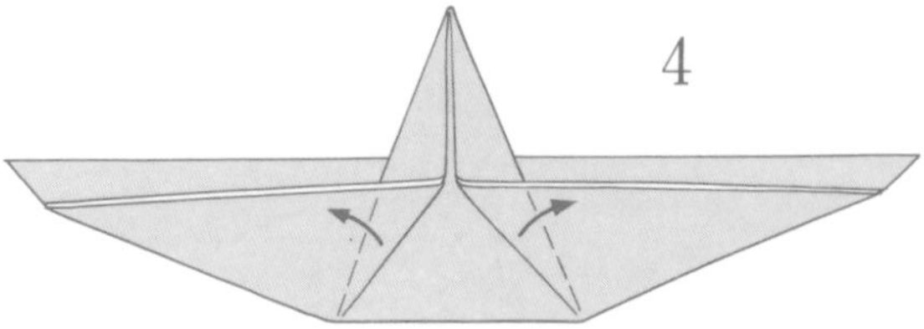

Fold open.

Open here.

5

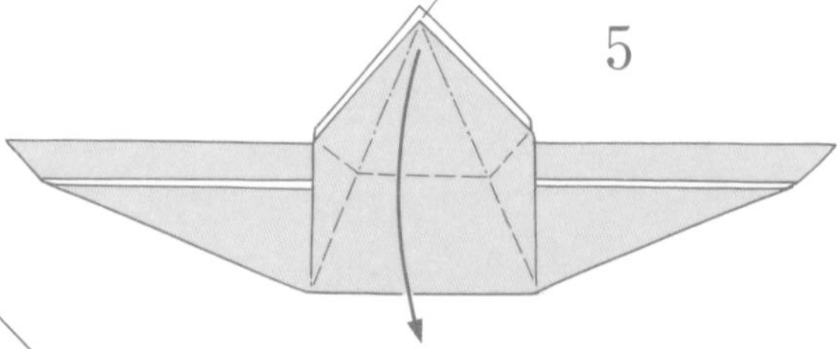

Folding top layer down, pull side paper in as in step 4.

Mid-step

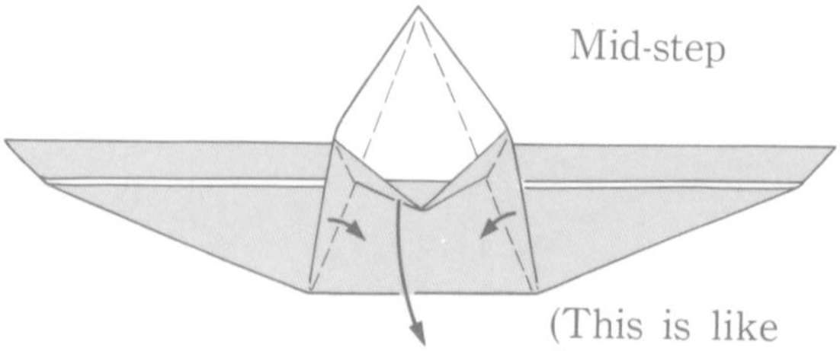

(This is like folding a Crane.)

2

1/3

6

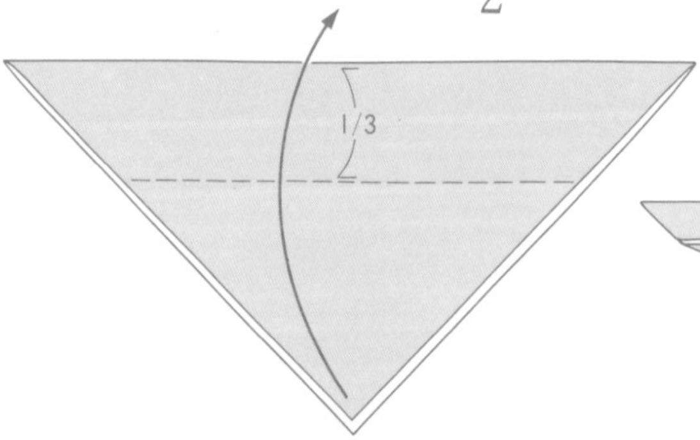

3

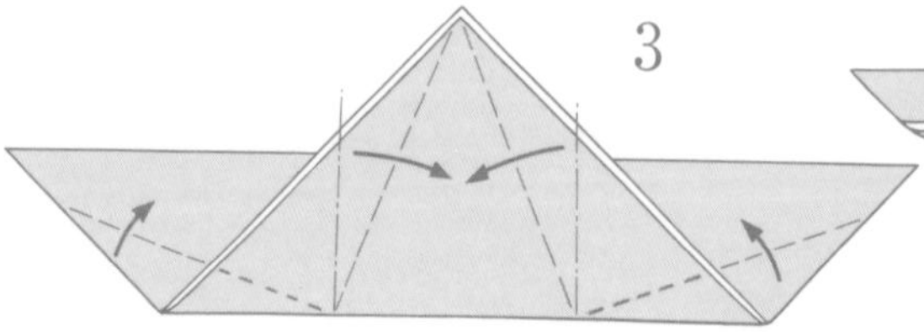

Gather paper from sides into center.

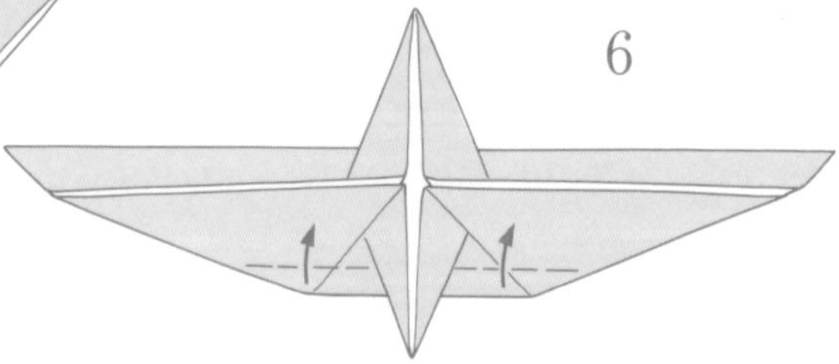

7

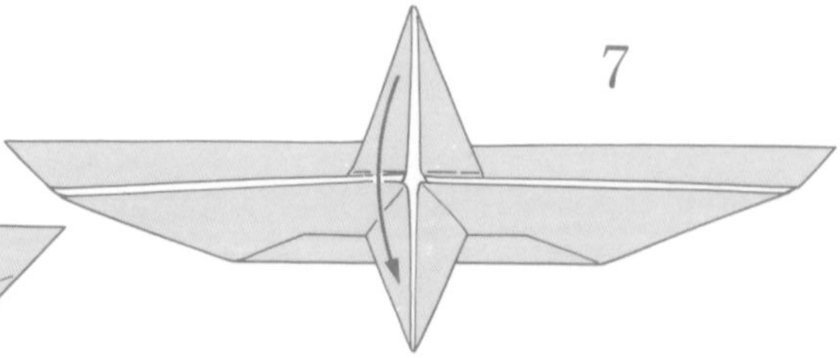

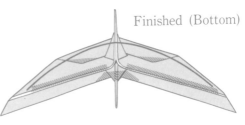

Finished (Bottom)

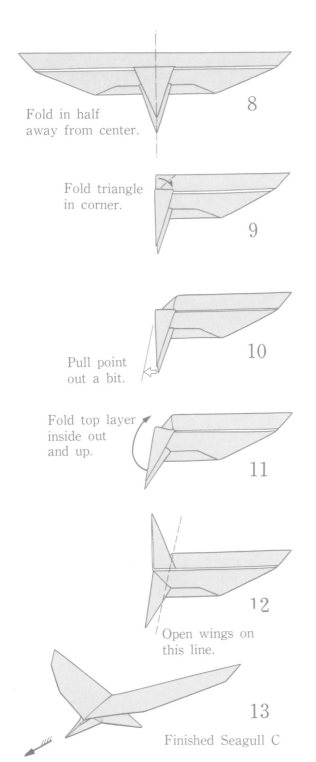

Fold in half
away from center.

8

Fold triangle
in corner.

9

Pull point
out a bit.

10

Fold top layer
inside out
and up.

11

12

Open wings on
this line.

13

Finished Seagull C

Adding a little glue to the parts shaded like this 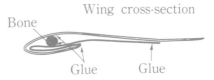 improves flight. If you bend the wings a bit, you can insert a bone for extra support. (Shown in diagram as a thick line.) Bones can be made out of cardboard and glued in (as shown in the wing cross-section diagram below). You can also have contests to see which birds stay in the air the longest!

Wing cross-section

Bone

Glue   Glue

In fact, using this kind of wing design on any of the birds described up to this point will help them to fly better. However, gluing adds an element of expansion and contraction which can decrease flying ability.

Japanese Stork

A variation on the Seagull, this is not quite the same folding sequence. Thinking about how to use the paper, and the new shape we want to make, we find the best way to create it.

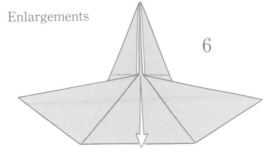

Enlargements

6

Open just enough to fold down one layer.

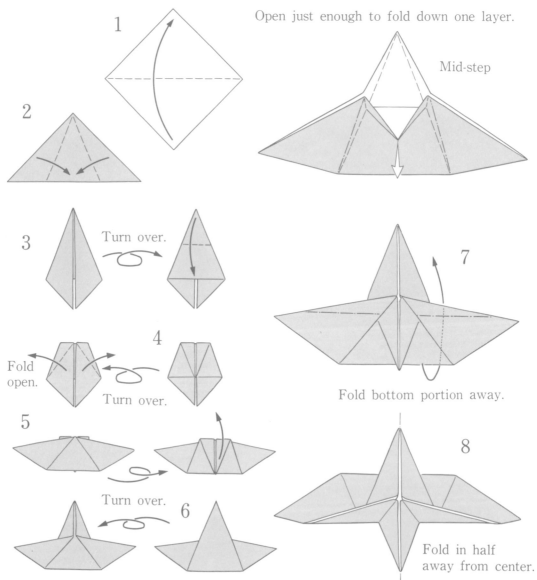

1

2

3   Turn over.

4

Fold open.   Turn over.

5

Turn over.   6

Mid-step

7

Fold bottom portion away.

8

Fold in half away from center.

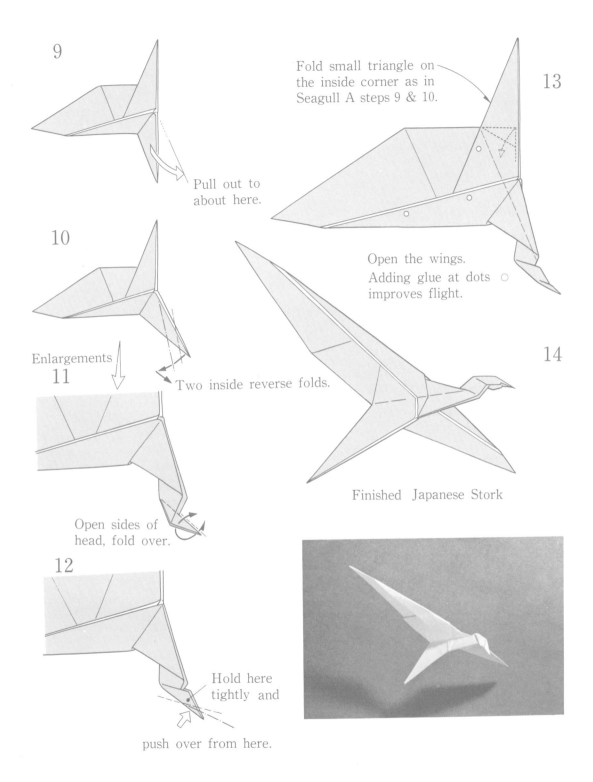

9

Pull out to about here.

10

Enlargements

11

Two inside reverse folds.

Open sides of head, fold over.

12

Hold here tightly and

push over from here.

13

Fold small triangle on the inside corner as in Seagull A steps 9 & 10.

Open the wings. Adding glue at dots ○ improves flight.

14

Finished Japanese Stork

Saberbill

This is a variation on the Seagull. The folding sequence and paper use are similar, but the relative size of the parts and the back side are different.

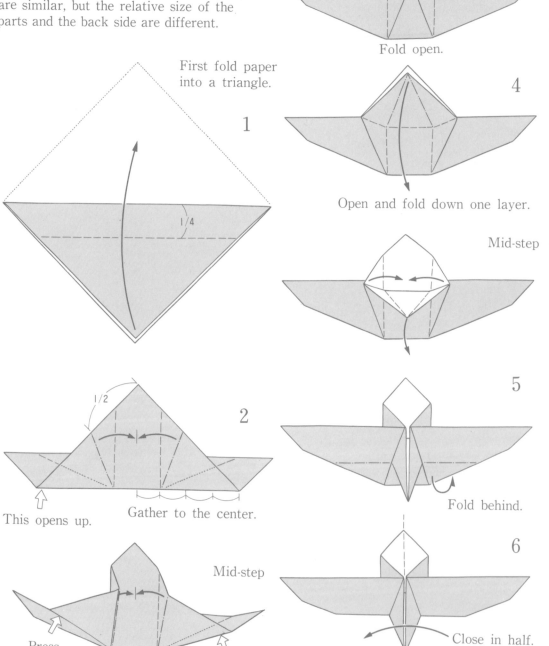

First fold paper into a triangle.

1

1/4

2

1/2

This opens up.

Gather to the center.

Press

Mid-step

3

Fold open.

4

Open and fold down one layer.

Mid-step

5

Fold behind.

6

Close in half.

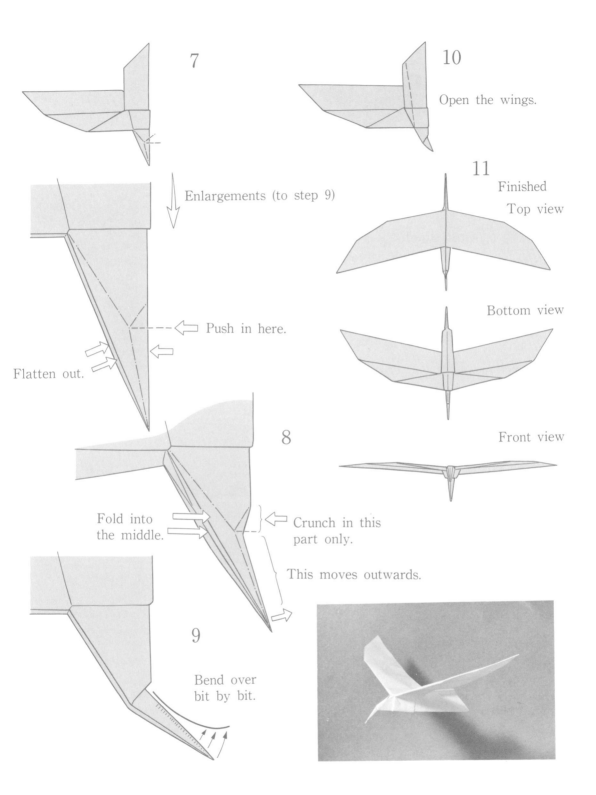

7

Enlargements (to step 9)

Push in here.

Flatten out.

8

Fold into
the middle.

Crunch in this
part only.

This moves outwards.

9

Bend over
bit by bit.

10

Open the wings.

11

Finished

Top view

Bottom view

Front view

Birds Made From Triangles
Paper Napkin Birds

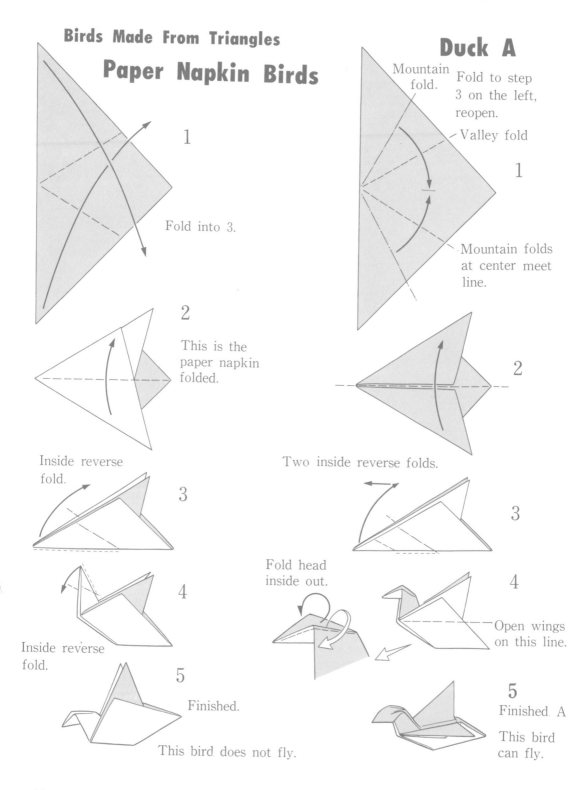

Duck A

1 Fold into 3.

2 This is the paper napkin folded.

Inside reverse fold.

3

4

Inside reverse fold.

5 Finished.

This bird does not fly.

Mountain fold.

Fold to step 3 on the left, reopen.

Valley fold

1

Mountain folds at center meet line.

2 Two inside reverse folds.

3

Fold head inside out.

4 Open wings on this line.

5 Finished A

This bird can fly.

Duck B

Aspects of Swan A are
applied here to Duck A.

From step 4 of Duck A.

1

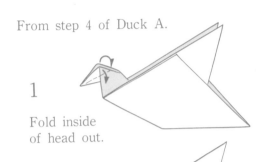

Fold inside
of head out.

2

Fold throat back
both sides.

3

Fold outside flaps.

4

Puff out head
for more realism.

Open wings.

5   Finished B

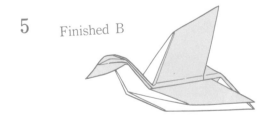

Duck C

From step 3 of
Duck A on pg. 54.

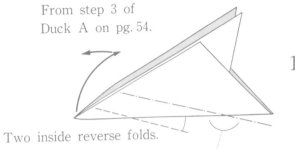

1

Two inside reverse folds.

This angle differs from the one on page 54.

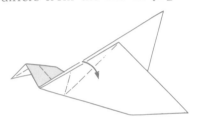

2

Hold here ● , pull
wings up a bit.

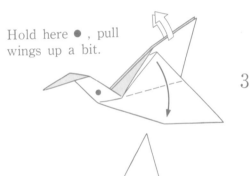

3

4

Finished C

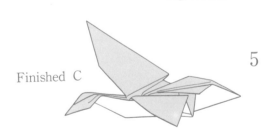

5

Water Fowl Origami Basics

These origami basics apply to long-necked, broad-winged water fowl like swans, wild geese, cranes and herons.

1 First cut a paper triangle.

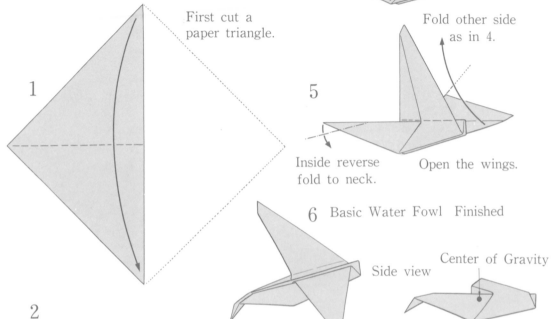

2 Fold up, fold other side away.

3 Leave this bit here. 1/2

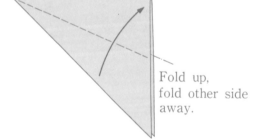

Twist inner bottom folds to front of wings.

4

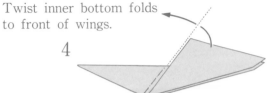

5 Fold other side as in 4.

Inside reverse fold to neck.

Open the wings.

6 Basic Water Fowl Finished

Side view

Center of Gravity

The shape is all right, but as the diagram shows, the area in front of the center of gravity, so it is not very stable, and does not fly well. A fold to the neck helps this a bit.

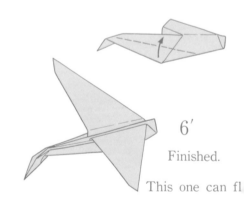

6' Finished.

This one can fl

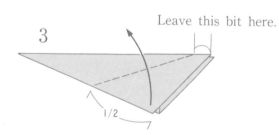

Swan C

(A variation on the left page)

(Cut paper into a triangle first)

Continued from step 5 on the left.

1

Unfold.

Fold both sides the same to step 6.

2 Fold down, make a mountain fold when you unfold. (Crimp on both sides.)

Outside reverse fold.

3

Fold on both sides.

Pull out inside paper.

Pull wings forward

4

Fold neck inside

5 Enlargements

Open, outside reverse fold.

6

Pull paper out from inside neck, fold on outside.

7

8

There are descriptions of neck folds on other pages so please apply them here.

9

Two inside reverse folds.

10

Finished

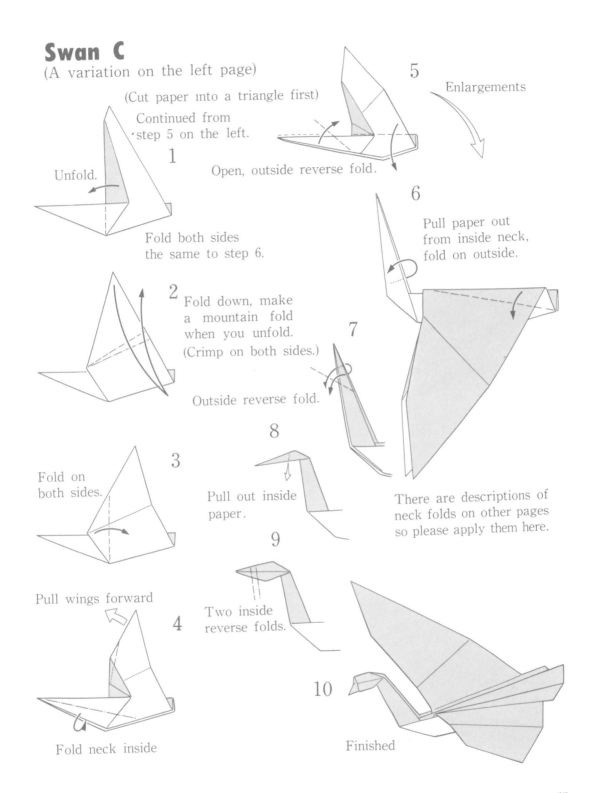

Black Sea Duck

In this variation on Swan C, the tail and wings are made first. In fact, origami folding order is often systematically turned back to front.

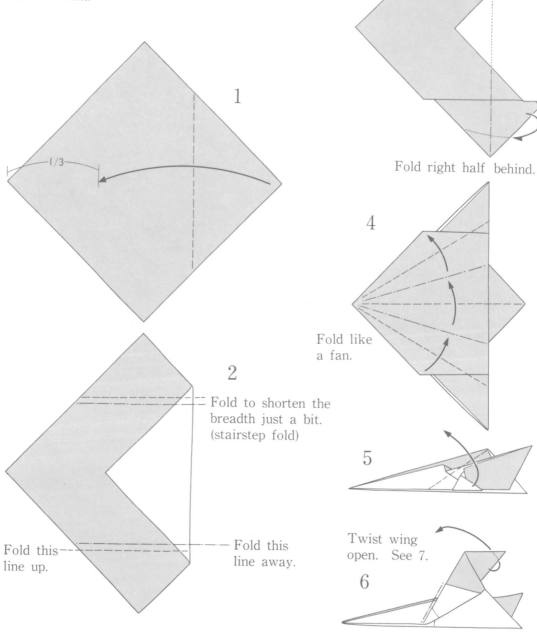

1

—1/3—

2

Fold to shorten the breadth just a bit. (stairstep fold)

Fold this line up.

Fold this line away.

3

Fold right half behind.

4

Fold like a fan.

5

6

Twist wing open. See 7.

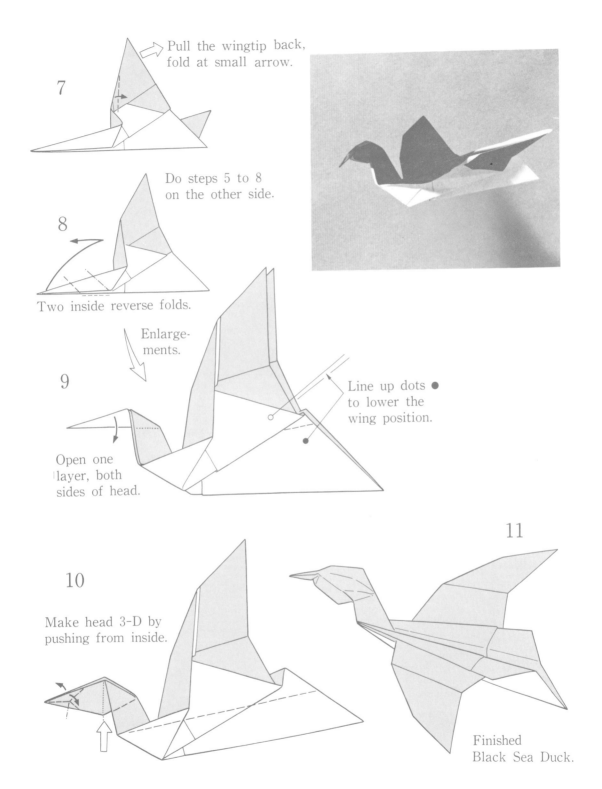

7

Pull the wingtip back, fold at small arrow.

Do steps 5 to 8 on the other side.

8

Two inside reverse folds.

Enlargements.

9

Line up dots ● to lower the wing position.

Open one layer, both sides of head.

11

10

Make head 3-D by pushing from inside.

Finished Black Sea Duck.

Folding Basics (Arranging wings, tails and heads)

No one knows who first created this Dove design, but it has always appeared in scores of origami books. It is so simple it is unclear exactly what bird it is supposed to be, but with a little help it can be made to fly.

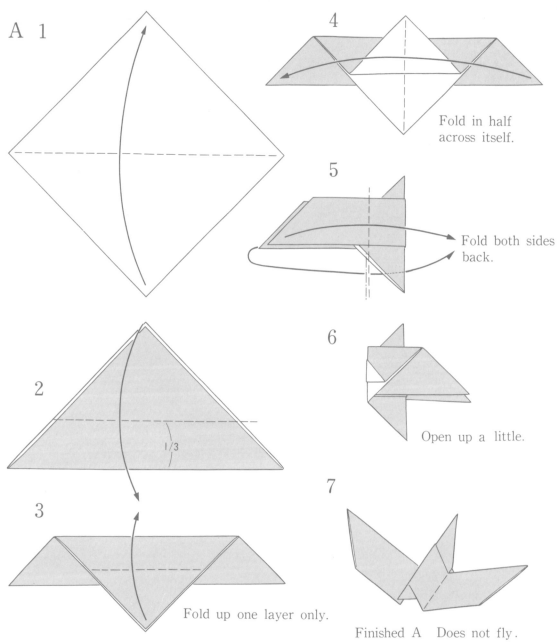

A 1

2

1/3

3

Fold up one layer only.

4

Fold in half across itself.

5

Fold both sides back.

6

Open up a little.

7

Finished A   Does not fly.

B A mountain fold at step 4 on the left inverts the body, but it cannot fly either.

C A and B cannot fly because their center of gravity is badly placed. This one can fly, because the center of gravity is further forward.

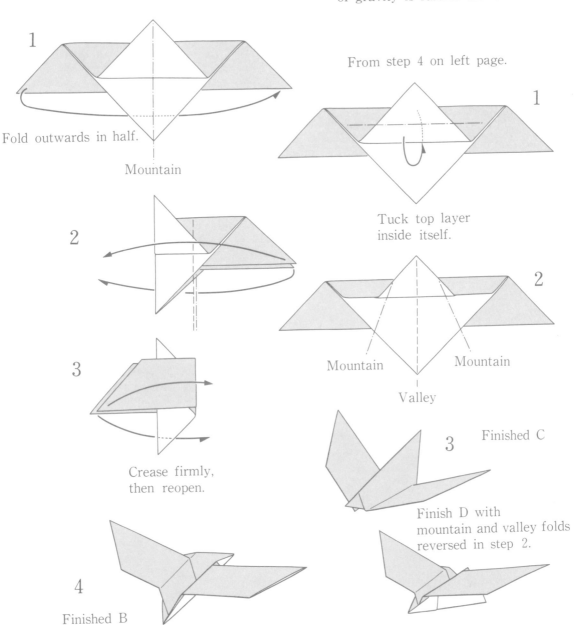

1

Fold outwards in half.

Mountain

From step 4 on left page.

1

Tuck top layer inside itself.

2

2

Mountain   Mountain

Valley

3

Crease firmly, then reopen.

3   Finished C

Finish D with mountain and valley folds reversed in step 2.

4

Finished B

Pale Ouzel (Shape-altering device)

These improvements to the birds from the previous page help to distinguish the front from the back.

First fold paper into a triangle.

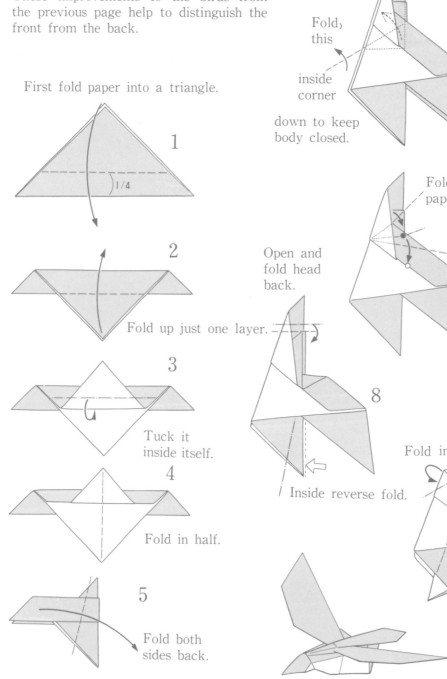

1

1/4

2

3

Tuck it inside itself.

4

Fold in half.

5

Fold both sides back.

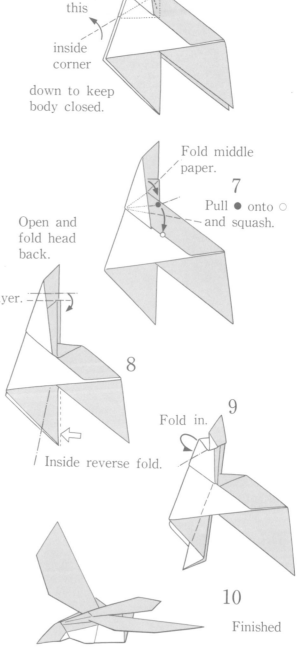

Enlargements

6

Fold this inside corner down to keep body closed.

Fold middle paper.

7

Pull ● onto ○ and squash.

Open and fold head back.

Fold up just one layer.

8

Inside reverse fold.

Fold in.

9

10

Finished

62

Ptarmigan

This bird, which lives in the high mountains of central Japan, is all white in winter except for a black spot in front of the eye. This design is a variation on the Ouzel.

From step 2 on the left

1

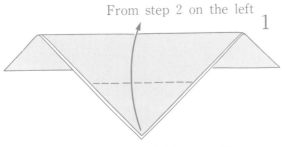

The top layer folds up with only a little showing above.

2

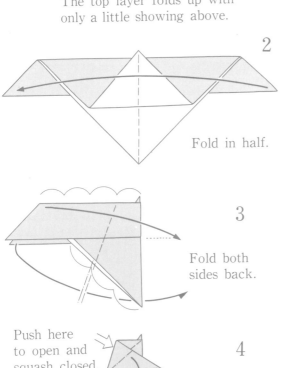

Fold in half.

3

Fold both sides back.

Push here to open and squash closed.

4

The — – – — line pulls paper back.

Mid-step

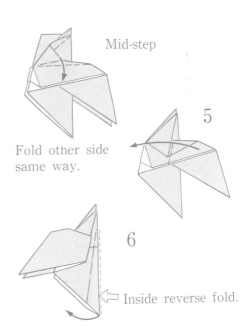

Fold other side same way.

5

6

Inside reverse fold.

7

Spread wings and tail.

8 Finished

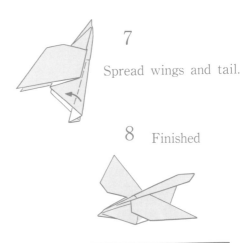

Siberian Blue Robin

The male of this small bird has a beautiful indigo back and white front. The folding order is a variation on the last page, beginning from step 3.

1

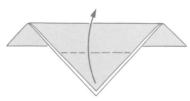

Fold up the top layer only, so just a bit sticks out above.

2

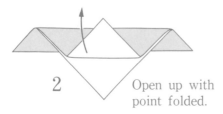

Open up with point folded.

3

4

5

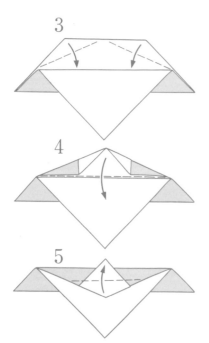

6

Mountain   Mountain
Valley

1/2

7

Fold this line over to gather paper in. Make a narrow fold to the bill at the same time.

Inside reverse fold.

8

Pull out inside paper.

9

Fold over, tuck back inside.

Spread tail and wings.

10

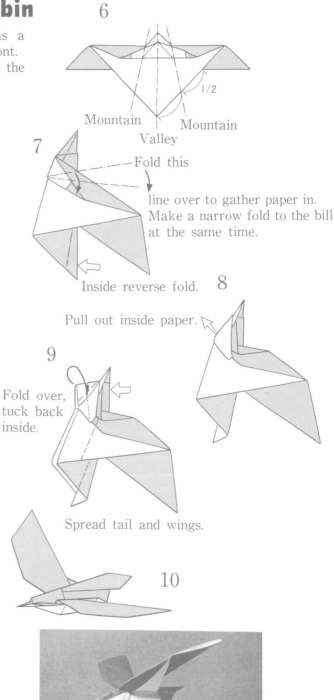

Shrike

The shrike, with its sharp beak and stout body, is a little bigger than a sparrow. A variation of the design on the last page, the folding order is more systematic. These folding order changes are one aspect of the art of origami.

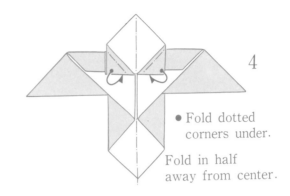

4

• Fold dotted corners under.

Fold in half away from center.

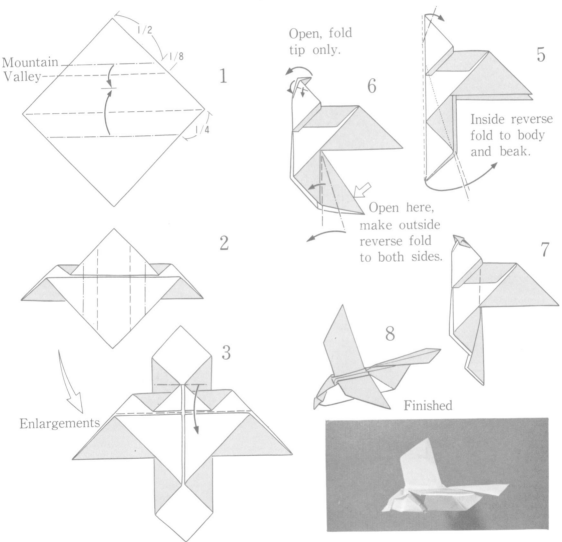

1

Mountain
Valley

1/2
1/8
1/4

2

Enlargements

3

Open, fold tip only.

6

Open here, make outside reverse fold to both sides.

5

Inside reverse fold to body and beak.

7

8

Finished

Woodpecker A

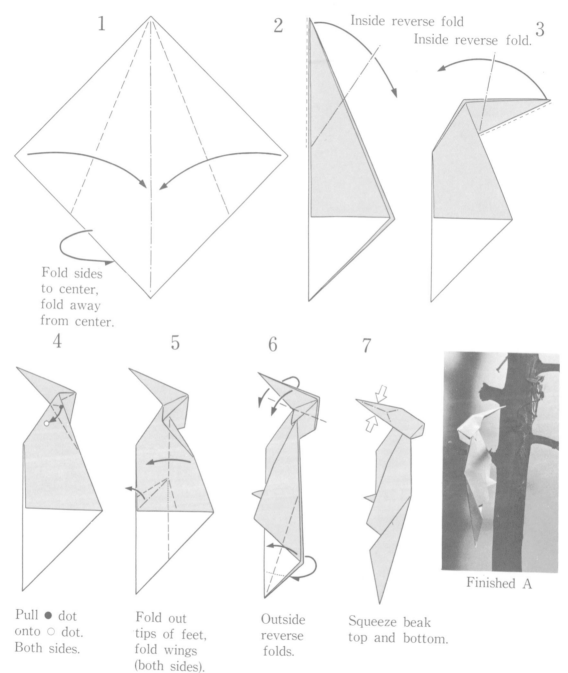

1

Fold sides
to center,
fold away
from center.

2

Inside reverse fold

3

Inside reverse fold.

4

Pull ● dot
onto ○ dot.
Both sides.

5

Fold out
tips of feet,
fold wings
(both sides).

6

Outside
reverse
folds.

7

Squeeze beak
top and bottom.

Finished A

This pattern does not fly.

Woodpecker B

The same as Woodpecker A but with added wings.

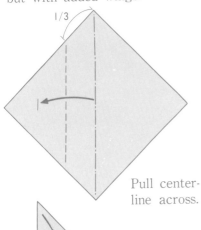

1/3

Pull center-line across.

2

3

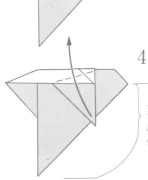

4

Fold bottom half as in steps 2-4, to match top half.

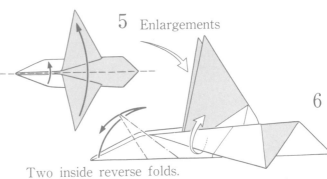

5 Enlargements

Two inside reverse folds.

6

Spread out layered paper.

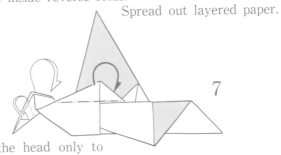

7

Return the head only to the way it was in step 6, turning it inside out.

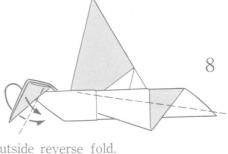

8

Outside reverse fold.

Open wings, tail along this line.

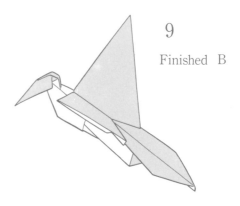

9

Finished B

Black Kite

Cut a square paper in half to make a rectangle.

To fold the wings.

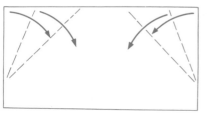

1

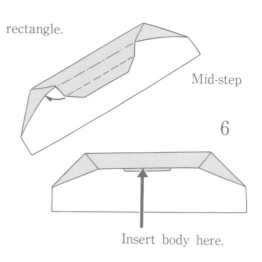

Mid-step

6

2

3

Roll one fold over the next.

4

Insert body here.

These wings fly well all on their own, so give them a try. They float like a butterfly, almost stalling mid-air.

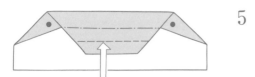

5

Fold and insert under paper with the dots.

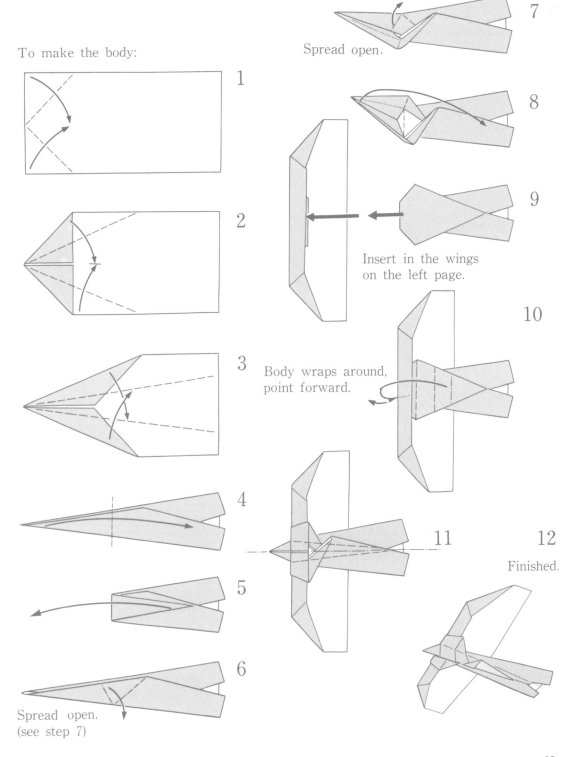

To make the body:

1

2

3

4

5

6

Spread open.
(see step 7)

7

Spread open.

8

9

Insert in the wings
on the left page.

10

Body wraps around,
point forward.

11

12

Finished.

69

About the author : Yoshihide Momotani

Yoshihide Momotani graduated in 1952 from Kyoto University with a B.Sc. in botany. After completing the liberal arts assistant professorship program at Tezukayama University, he became a professor in biological science at University of Osaka Prefecture, where he taught until taking early retirement from the university in 1992. He continues to teach molecular biology at Phillips University Japan. He has a Ph.D. in Science, is a pharmicist, a member of the Japanese Botanical Society, a member of the Bio-Physics Society and president of Origami International Japan (address: c/o The Momotani Family, 30-5, Noda 3-chome, Kuzuha, Hirakata-shi, Osaka-fu, 573 Japan). His origami creations have been published in the Asahi Newspaper since 1970 and in the Sankei Newspaper since 1974, and information about his origami work was broadcast on Asahi TV in 1973 and on NHK TV in 1974. Exhibitions of his original works have been held in many countries over the past decade, 3 to 5 times a year, including both large and small displays. The most recent large exhibition was held at the International Youth Library in Munich in 1991. In the case of his exhibitions held in Japan, a section is sometimes devoted to the works of overseas origami enthusiasts.

A book of Professor Momotani's original origami works was first published in 1971, and since then 22 other such books have been released. Although his many readers around the world cannot read Japanese, they fold his origami models by following the diagrams in his books. This new text is a complete translation of the 1986 revised edition of the book first published in 1977 by Seibundo Shinkosha Publishing Co., Ltd.